CULTURE SHOCK!

Beijing
At your Door

KAY JONES • ANTHONY PAN

Graphic Arts Center Publishing Company
Portland, Oregon

In the same series

Argentina	*Ecuador*	*Laos*	*Sri Lanka*
Australia	*Egypt*	*Malaysia*	*Sweden*
Austria	*Finland*	*Mauritius*	*Switzerland*
Belgium	*France*	*Mexico*	*Syria*
Bolivia	*Germany*	*Morocco*	*Taiwan*
Borneo	*Greece*	*Myanmar*	*Thailand*
Brazil	*Hong Kong*	*Nepal*	*Turkey*
Britain	*Hungary*	*Netherlands*	*UAE*
California	*India*	*Norway*	*Ukraine*
Canada	*Indonesia*	*Pakistan*	*USA*
Chile	*Iran*	*Philippines*	*USA—The South*
China	*Ireland*	*Saudi Arabia*	*Venezuela*
Costa Rica	*Israel*	*Scotland*	*Vietnam*
Cuba	*Italy*	*Singapore*	
Czech Republic	*Japan*	*South Africa*	
Denmark	*Korea*	*Spain*	

Barcelona At Your Door	*Paris At Your Door*	*A Student's Guide*
Beijing At Your Door	*Rome At Your Door*	*A Traveller's Medical*
Chicago At Your Door	*San Francisco At Your*	*Guide*
Havana At Your Door	*Door*	*A Wife's Guide*
Jakarta At Your Door	*Shanghai At Your Door*	*Living and Working*
Kuala Lumpur, Malaysia	*Tokyo At Your Door*	*Abroad*
At Your Door	*Vancouver At Your Door*	*Personal Protection At*
London At Your Door		*Home & Abroad*
Moscow At Your Door	*A Globe-Trotter's Guide*	*Working Holidays*
Munich At Your Door	*A Parent's Guide*	*Abroad*
New York At Your Door		

Front cover photograph by Focus Team
Back cover photograph by The Hutchison Library
Illustrations by TRIGG

© 2003 Times Media Private Limited

This book is published by special
arrangement with Times Media Private Limited
Times Centre, 1 New Industrial Road, Singapore 536196
International Standard Book Number 1-55868-691-6
Library of Congress Catalog Number 20-02102708
Graphic Arts Center Publishing Company
P.O. Box 10306 • Portland, Oregon 97296-0306 • (503) 226-2402

Printed in Singapore

To Bernadette Pan

CONTENTS

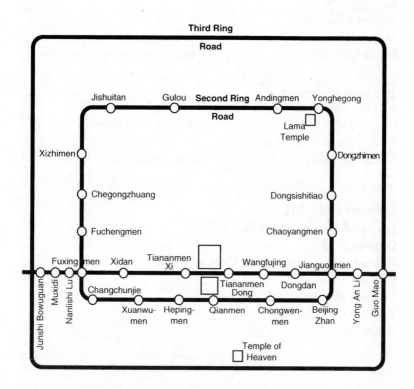

Map of Beijing subway stops inside the Third Ring Road.

ACKNOWLEDGMENTS

We are greatly indebted to the following people for their assistance in creating this book about life in Beijing:

First and foremost, we are grateful to Lynn Witham for originally suggesting us to the publisher, and for her relentless efforts to turn our writings into something readable. As always, she was a strong source of moral support.

Long-time friend Walter Stryker, who has lived in Beijing for about two decades and who speaks excellent Mandarin, drafted certain portions of this book. He gave generously of his time for discussions, edits, and comments on many issues when his calendar was already full.

Jeff Minard was an early volunteer in the editing process, and read more than one version of the manuscript. He also assisted with the Internet resources listed toward the end of the book. Chris Cooper gave us feedback on a draft and took several of the photographs that appear in these pages.

We received much support from our colleagues Hu Wenzhong and Cornelius Grove, who are the authors of *Encountering the Chinese* (details about this book are listed in Further Reading). In particular, Professor Hu offered well-chosen and extremely insightful comments.

Eric Ryan helped by distributing draft copies to volunteer readers. In Beijing, Zhang Xiaozhou was a wonderful guide to certain aspects of Beijing culture, and he provided several updates, details, and embellishments for this book. Russ Miller, an active member of the Rotary group in Beijing, introduced us to several people whom we interviewed during the research process.

Other people who contributed to our research and editing were Bob and Carol Gates, Diane Russell and her husband

Nakagome Toshiyoshi, Kidder Smith, Roberta Lipson, Isabel Liu, Zhao Mailu, Kelly Lau, Dr. Larry Gee, Peter Crowhurst, Dr. Peter Yu, and Tina Castillo. Friends and family who read drafts and gave us feedback include Roland and Nancy Jones, Amy Frankel, and Nick Fono.

Hosts of other people were gracious in offering advice and support in the process of writing this book. We wish we could mention each of them individually.

It would not have been possible to complete this project without the assistance of each of these wonderful, patient people. In the end, only we saw the final draft; whatever errors and omissions remain are our own. We just hope that our love for the city of Beijing shines through in the pages of this book.

Kay Jones
Anthony Pan

INTRODUCTION

Beijing is an amazing city. It has been transformed over the last 20 years into a world-class metropolis. High-rise buildings now tower above historical sites, and the airport accommodates both international as well as domestic travelers in style and comfort. Even some of the old main roads, once filled with automobiles, bicycles, lumbering trucks, sheep, pedestrians, buses, tricycle flatbeds, and horse-drawn carts, have become relatively uncluttered modern highways.

This book is all about thriving during an extended stay in the modern city of Beijing. We hope it will be useful to a wide range of people planning to move there—to Asians, including people from Hong Kong and "returning" Chinese; to Westerners; and to any other English-speaking foreigners anticipating such a move. Each group will experience Beijing in a different way.

In this book, we use three different terms to distinguish newcomers to Beijing. The most comprehensive term that we use is "outsider," which is similar to the Mandarin term *waidiren* (literally, "outside place people"). Although "outsider" is used here to mean anyone who is not originally from Beijing, Chinese people primarily use this term to refer to Chinese people from other parts of China. This is because Chinese people, among themselves, are acutely aware of regional variations within China in terms of culture and differences in dialect. Anyone who is an "outsider" or *waidiren* will have to make some effort to adapt in Beijing.

Another more exclusive term that we use in this book is "expat." Short for "expatriate," this term refers to people who have moved to Beijing from other countries and Chinese territories. Expats are thus a subset of "outsiders." Although it is possible to translate "expat" into Chinese, the term is mostly used in English by foreign residents in order to distinguish themselves from foreign visitors and tourists. In other words, the term "expat" does not include people from other Chinese cities who go to live in Beijing, but it includes people from Hong Kong (a territory of China known as an SAR or Special Administrative Region).

The third and most narrowly defined term that we use in this book is "foreigner," which is usually translated in Mandarin as *waiguoren* (literally, "outside country people"). Here it is used in the same manner generally used by Chinese people to mean "non-Chinese people." (Mandarin speakers also use *waiguoren* to mean "non-Asians" or, more frequently, "Westerners.") Foreigners are a subset of expats; both expats and foreigners are outsiders.

Within these pages, we tackle issues of adjustment and adaptation. How can outsiders make sense of this place? How do they make the most of living in a city with such a rich historical and cultural heritage? With the relatively high levels of pollution in Beijing, how do they keep their bodies healthy so their minds can function? How do they make Beijing feel like "home"?

This book is intended as a guide to adaptation to life in Beijing, certain aspects of which have not changed much in recent years. In our experience, these are the aspects to which outsiders usually have the most difficulty adjusting, precisely because they are cultural "institutions" and are unlikely to change in the near future. When one day you realize that you understand and even appreciate these cultural institutions, that is when Beijing will become "home."

One of the first aspects to which outsiders must adjust is that change is a permanent feature of Beijing. It is undergoing upheaval on a daily basis, not only in general pursuit of modernization, but also in preparation for the 2008 Summer Olympics. The change is so rapid that an entire neighborhood sometimes disappears overnight. Consequently, this book is not intended as a reference to the latest restaurants, hotels, clubs, or stores, although some old standbys have been included. We hope they will still be there when you are ready to experience them.

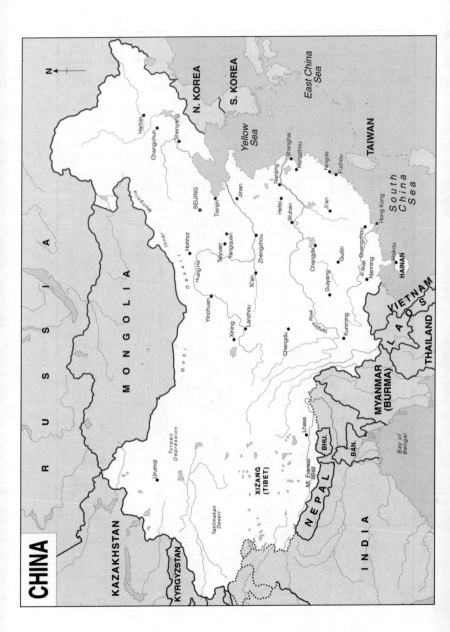

CHINA

13

City Map of Beijing

Chapter One

WELCOME TO BEIJING

Beijing has changed dramatically since China opened its doors and expats first arrived in relatively large numbers in the early 1980s. Back then, the expats who survived were those who were adept at creating their own entertainment. After all, a substantial portion of the day was consumed by waiting in line for taxis or for access to a hotel telex machine. Diplomats and journalists could live in apartments, but the only choice for other expats was hotel rooms. Most restaurants in the city were State-run, served mediocre food, and closed by 7 p.m. or earlier. If you hadn't managed to eat by then, you survived on whatever rations you had squirreled away in your hotel room or office drawer. Entertainment for expats was essentially limited to the TGIF

(Thank Goodness It's Friday) parties at the Western embassies. The Jianguo Hotel (the first joint venture hotel in the city) became the expat oasis — its coffee shop was open past 8 p.m.!

Sadly, some of the old features of Beijing that eventually endeared themselves to expats, such as the open-air markets and bustling *hutong* (residential lanes), are disappearing. But these days, Beijing has myriad other ways of entertaining its foreign visitors. There is so much to see and do — movies and museums; parks and pagodas; martial arts and motorcycling are all available. Residents of the city can now fuel up on caffeine at one of several Starbucks cafés in town. What more could an expat want from life? The amenities for expats living in Beijing far outnumber those found in other Chinese cities. Those who live there and travel around China express feelings of relief and appreciation when they return "home."

Writers like to comment on how quickly Beijing is rebuilding and modernizing; the great number of construction sites in the city leads English speakers to joke that the crane is the official bird of Beijing. But the ride toward modernization is often a bumpy one, and the more one rushes, the more one feels the bumps. Expats who live here come to realize that there are two sides to this city. On the one hand, many of the *hutong* of Beijing are being replaced by tall, modern-looking buildings. On the other hand, many people in Beijing still do not have running water in their homes. Gleaming shopping malls offer expensive foreign goods for sale, and on the weekends the stores are packed with shoppers. Watch closely, though. How many actually buy something? Most of these imported goods are far too dear for the local citizenry.

Approximately 60% of China's population still lives in rural areas. Some urban dwellers and certainly a large portion of the manual laborers temporarily living in cities are not even one generation removed from rural life. This leaves many Chinese cities, including Beijing, striving to accommodate the juxtaposition of the rustic tendencies of their populations and the modern initiatives of their governments. Outsiders who travel or move to Beijing from rural settings can be intimidated by its sleekness, perhaps staring upward at its tall buildings or hesitating before gingerly stepping onto escalators.

In contrast, expats accustomed to the urban environments of nations that industrialized much earlier than China could find certain features of Beijing unwelcoming, such as its occasional open manholes, pipes laying across sidewalks, and a few *hutong* that are too narrow for all but the smallest cars. Here and there, rural life spills into the city. Although horse-drawn carts are officially banned except in the wee hours of the morning, it is occasionally possible to witness a horse-drawn "honey wagon" that has wandered into the city in search of fertilizer before 11

The entrance to the Forbidden City sits at the north end of Tiananmen Square.

17

p.m. (For those who are not familiar with this rural expression, a "honey wagon" is a mode of transporting excrement—in this case, of human origin.)

All that said, standing in Tiananmen Square—considered by most to be the center of Beijing—induces feelings of awe in many outsiders. Facing the Forbidden City, the Great Hall of the People rises to your left. Chairman Mao's Mausoleum and Qianmen (the front gate of the old city wall) peer over your shoulder, with the Museum of the Chinese Revolution rising to your right. At some point, we're sure that every foreign resident assumes this position, looks around, and mutters to her- or himself, "Wow. I live here."

Welcome to Beijing!

BEIJING: "CENTER" OF CHINA

As with many other world capitals, people alternately use "Beijing" to refer to China's capital city and to refer to the country's government. Beijing is the center of political power; the center of intellectual activity; the center of international trade and foreign relations. Chinese people around the country are reminded every day of Beijing's leadership, as they are obligated to set their clocks to match those in the capital. When the time of day is mentioned on the radio in cities as far away as Lanzhou (in the western province of Gansu), announcers always say, "Beijing time is... (2 p.m., for example)." It's a subtle reminder to China's citizens that Beijing establishes the tempo to which the rest of the country should march. When you live in Beijing, you feel like everyone else in China is just a little out of step and just a little less mindful of political realities.

To see Beijing in the context of China as a whole, take a look at the map on page 13. Most of the areas identified on this map are provinces, such as Liaoning and Sichuan, and are inhabited primarily by Han people (Han means "ethnically Chinese," and in modern China, this term is often used to distinguish Chinese people from the members of 55 official ethnic minority groups. Mongols and Manchus are two of these minorities.) Taiwan has been included because, from the perspective of the government of the People's Republic of China, the island of Taiwan is a province of China. Five areas—Xinjiang, Tibet, Inner Mongolia, Guangxi, and Ningxia—are called "autonomous regions" and are inhabited mostly by ethnic minorities.

Four of the areas—Beijing, Shanghai, Chongqing, and Tianjin—are "autonomous cities"; they are not part of any province and are usually referred to in English as "municipalities." Their ruling bodies, such as the Beijing Municipal Government and the Shanghai Municipal Government, report directly to the central government of China, rather than to a provincial body. The governments of Macau and Hong Kong, which are Special Administrative Regions (SAR) of China, also report directly to the central government but maintain unique legal and economic systems. (Hong Kong was a British colony that reverted to Chinese rule in 1997; Macau was a Portuguese colony that reverted to Chinese rule in 1999.)

For your reference, the Mandarin pronunciation of each of these designations and place names is listed in the *Glossary*.

HISTORICAL TOUR OF BEIJING

"Middle Kingdom"

China has the longest history of any society still in existence today. Much earlier than neighboring societies, China developed a written language, sophisticated philosophies, historical records, formal rites, social rituals, and a bureaucratic system of government. To the early inhabitants of China, the people of neighboring societies seemed less refined or less civilized. Thinking that China must be at the center of the world and that it should be a model for other

19

societies, Chinese people called their nation *zhongguo*, meaning "center country" — a term often translated as "middle kingdom."

The belief among Chinese people that their society is the most civilized in the world is still quite prevalent today. A list of modern Chinese values developed in one research project includes "sense of cultural superiority." The people of Beijing follow this general tendency and, in addition, sometimes consider themselves more civilized than other Chinese people. If China was the center of the world, then Beijing must have been the center of China. The city has been the national capital and the vortex of Chinese political, intellectual, social, and cultural currents for about seven centuries, but its history goes back much further.

Ancient Times
The region around Beijing has historical roots dating back as far as a half-million years, as evidenced by the remains of Peking Man (a prehistoric human). These remains were found in the late 1920s in a village called Zhoukoudian, located about 34 miles (54.72 km) southwest of present-day Beijing. Estimates of the age of artifacts discovered there range from 200,000 to almost 500,000 years. The village is now the site of a museum where many of these artifacts can be seen. .

Later anthropological finds include evidence of human settlement within the modern borders of Beijing, dating back 20,000 years. There is other evidence of human settlement in the region dating from about 5,000 years ago, reflecting Beijing's historical significance as a center of trade among people in the central plain (Yellow River area) of north China and nomadic tribes roaming on the other side of mountains to the north. The nomadic tribes, however, would sometimes turn from friendly trading partners into threatening invaders. Beijing had early defensive significance for China because of its strategic location near mountain passes from where the nomads were likely to attack.

At times it was overpowered and captured, serving as a capital for some of these nomadic groups, while the Chinese (Han) capitals were usually located to the south or southeast of modern Beijing.

In the Warring States period (403–221 B.C.), the state of Yan dominated the region and designated the city of Ji (located just east of the present city of Beijing) as its capital. Ji was often referred to as Yanjing, which means "Capital of Yan," or literally, "Capital of Swallows." Several popular locations, organizations and products in Beijing today carry the brand name, Yanjing. In addition to Beijing Beer, for example, Yanjing Beer is a popular brand. At one time, a prominent academic institution in Beijing was named Yanjing University (Yanjing is also sometimes spelled "Yenching"); it merged with Beijing University in 1952.

Over several decades, many of the mountain passes and other strategic points north of Beijing were fortified against invaders coming from the areas later known as Mongolia and Manchuria. These fortifications were connected during the Qin Dynasty (221–206 B.C.) to form the eastern portion of the Great Wall. (A dynasty denotes an historical period in which an empire is governed by members of a single family. The name of the dynasty was usually chosen by the founder.)

In later centuries, the people of Beijing must have suffered from identity crisis, as the name of the city was changed several times. When north China was ruled by Khitans (nomad Mongol) during the Liao Dynasty (907–1125), their primary capital was farther north and Beijing was referred to as Nanjing or "South Capital." When the Tatar Jurchen from Manchuria took control during the Jin Dynasty (1115–1234), Beijing was successively called Nandu (another way of saying "South Capital") and Zhongdu, or "Center Capital."

In 1215, under the leadership of Genghis Khan, the Mongols attacked Zhongdu and destroyed the city. During the Yuan Dynasty (1206–1368), Genghis Khan's grandson, Kublai Khan, decided to rebuild the city as his winter capital and named it Dadu, or "Great Capital." Dadu is another term that is still used today for places in and products made in Beijing.

Although built by Mongols, Dadu was designed to include an imperial palace surrounded by streets in a grid pattern. This was the place that so enthralled the Venetian traveller Marco Polo when he visited China in the late 13th century. In fact, his description of the city and of Chinese inventions such as paper money left many Europeans in disbelief. However, the city that Marco Polo saw is not the Beijing that people see today, for that city (most of which lay to the north of today's Forbidden City) was later rebuilt during the Ming Dynasty (1368–1644). Visit the Confucius Temple just west of the Lama Temple for some fine examples of Yuan architectural style. (Confucius was a philosopher living in the sixth century B.C. He proposed a system of ethics which, using the family as a model, defined the roles and responsibilities of different members of society.)

With the founding of the Ming Dynasty, the capital was moved to the location of today's city of Nanjing (in Jiangsu Province), and Beijing's status was relegated to that of a provincial town. It was renamed Beiping or "North Peace," an appellation that was also used during the 1900s and is sometimes used in Taiwan today to refer to Beijing. (Visitors from Taiwan should take special care to refrain from referring to the capital by this name.)

Beijing the Capital
In 1403, one of the Ming emperors' sons seized the throne, assumed the ruling name Yongle, and established the city as China's capital, renaming it Beijing (North Capital). This was the first and only time that Beijing was the capital of a Han imperial empire. The city was rebuilt and essentially became the metropolitan city which we know today.

In rebuilding the city, the Ming government applied Chinese cosmological principles, designing the capital as a microcosm of the universe. This configuration included a series of concentric squares, with the city wall at the perimeter and the Forbidden City at the center. The emperor resided at the center of this "universe." The Forbidden City, along with other Ming architectural landmarks, such as the Temple of Heaven, remain prominent features of Beijing today.

A throne in the Forbidden City awaits visitors.

Concerned with the perennial threat of nomadic invasion from the north, Yongle also decided to reconstruct the Great Wall, which had fallen into disrepair since its original construction in the third century B.C. Much of the Great Wall that tourists see today, such as the Badaling section, was first restored during the Ming Dynasty. Returning to Beijing from a visit to the Great Wall, visitors also often stop by to see the Ming Tombs, a few of which have been excavated. Thirteen (out of 17) Ming emperors are buried there, along with many of their wives and concubines.

The Badaling section of the Great Wall is the one most tourists visit.

The Ming Dynasty came to an end as peasant rebels captured the city and the emperor hanged himself from a tree on Coal Hill (inside Jingshan Park, just north of the Forbidden City). Within weeks, the rebels themselves were vanquished by Manchu invaders. Beijing once again became the capital of a China under foreign rule—the capital of the Qing Dynasty (1644–1912). In fact, these Manchu rulers took pride in tracing their ancestral roots to the Jurchen who had conquered Beijing in the 12th century.

The transition in rule was a traumatic experience for Beijing's residents. The Manchus declared that the northern part of the city, where all of the government buildings and residences were located and surrounded by the city wall, would be the exclusive domain of the Manchus. Han (Chinese) people living there were forced to vacate their residences and move to the bustling commercial district on the southern edge of the city. This neighborhood comprised most of the territory currently known as the Xuanwu and Chongwen Districts. (Refer to the section on the *Districts of Beijing* for more information.)

There were long periods of peace and prosperity for Beijing during the rule of the Qing Dynasty, and especially under two emperors — Kangxi, who reigned from 1661–1722 and Qianlong, who reigned from 1735–1796. Like the Mongol rulers who preceded the Ming Dynasty, these Manchu rulers patronized Buddhism. The Lama Temple, located just inside the northeast corner of the old city wall, was built by Kangxi and is said to have been used later by Qianlong as a resting place for his father's remains.

During the early years of the Qing Dynasty, Chinese rulers sought the guidance of Jesuit astronomers in order to make a more accurate lunar calendar and to better predict natural phenomena such as eclipses. This was important to the imperial rulers because, according to traditional Chinese thinking, astronomical phenomena can have a tremendous impact on human affairs. Evidence of the scientific teachings of the Jesuit

The Ancient Observatory sits atop an old section of the Beijing city wall.

25

missionaries can be viewed at the Ancient Observatory on the south side of Beijing.

Qing emperors were responsible for building two other famous sites: Yuanmingyuan (known to many foreigners as the Old Summer Palace) and the Summer Palace that most tourists visit today. Both of these are situated to the northwest of the city of Beijing. Unfortunately, both sites were attacked by Western forces in the late 1800s, and Yuanmingyuan was virtually destroyed. On display at the Summer Palace is the pride of the Empress Dowager Cixi—a lovely, but essentially useless, marble boat.

TIMELINE OF CHINESE DYNASTIES

23rd–18th century B.C.	Xia (Hsia) Dynasty
18th–11th century B.C.	Shang Dynasty
11th century–770 B.C.	Western Zhou (Chou) Dynasty
771–256 B.C.	Eastern Zhou (Chou) Dynasty / Spring and Autumn Period
403–221 B.C.	Warring States Period
221–206 B.C.	Qin (Ch'in) Dynasty
202 B.C.–A.D. 220	Han Dynasty
A.D. 220 - 280	Three Kingdoms Period
A.D. 265 - 316	Western Jin (Chin) Dynasty
A.D. 317 - 420	Eastern Jin (Chin) Dynasty
A.D. 420 - 589	Northern and Southern Dynasties
A.D. 589 - 618	Sui Dynasty
A.D. 618 - 907	Tang (T'ang) Dynasty
A.D. 907 - 979	Five Dynasties and Ten Kingdoms
A.D. 916 - 1125	Liao Dynasty (*Khitan*)
A.D. 960 - 1279	Song (Sung) Dynasty
A.D. 1126 - 1234	Jin (Chin) Dynasty (*Tatar Jurchen*)
A.D. 1279 - 1368	Yuan Dynasty (*Mongol*)
A.D. 1368 - 1644	Ming Dynasty
A.D. 1644 - 1911	Qing (Ch'ing) Dynasty (*Manchu*)

NAVIGATING BEIJING

Beijing is relatively easy to get around once you orient yourself by using the Second and Third Ring Roads. (An additional Fourth Ring Road traverses the suburbs, and a Fifth Ring Road is in the works.) The map below shows the general layout of these arteries and several landmarks. To give you an idea of the geographical size of the city, the Third Ring Road (Sanhuan Lu) is approximately 9 miles (14 kilometers) square. The inner loop around the city, the Second Ring Road (Erhuan Lu), follows the old city inner wall; the gate names refer to the old gates of that wall, most of which are no longer standing.

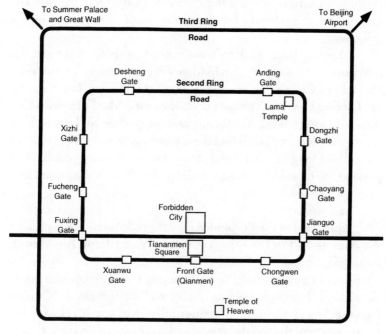

Map showing the layout of Beijing.

Many newcomers find it confusing that the names of some Beijing roads change in relation to the old city gates. The road that goes between the Forbidden City and Tiananmen Square is a good example — the portion shown on the map has six names. With some keys, though, the naming system is easy to understand. Here is the first key:

men = gate

wai = outside

nei = inside

Thus, Jianguomenwai Avenue is the section of the road that leads "outside," or away from, the city starting at the Jianguo Gate. Jianguomennei Avenue is the section of road that leads "inside" the city, or toward the Forbidden City, from the Jianguo Gate. (See the *Glossary* for assistance in pronouncing Chinese syllables.)

Moving from east to west, about midway between the Jianguo Gate and the Forbidden City, the name of the road changes to Chang An Avenue. (Chang An means "Long Peace" or "Lasting Peace.") The portion to the east of the Forbidden City is called Dong Chang An Avenue and the portion to the west is Xi Chang An Avenue. You'll find these words in two of the gate names as well — Dongzhi Gate and Xizhi Gate. In case you haven't guessed the meaning of these words by now, here is the second key:

dong = east

xi = west

Thus, east of the Forbidden City the road name is East Chang An Avenue and to the west it is called West Chang An Avenue. From Xi Chang An Avenue, still continuing west, the name changes to Fuxingmennei (Inside Fuxing Gate) Avenue; crossing the second ring road, the name becomes Fuxingmenwai (Outside Fuxing Gate) Avenue. (Incidentally, for some reason, the combination of the words for east and west (*dongxi*) means "thing." Your Chinese vocabulary is increasing exponentially!)

As long as we're discussing directions, let's add two more. The *bei* in Beijing means "north," so the name of the city literally means "north capital." *Nan* means "south," hence the name Nanjing means "south capital." (See the *Glossary* for the Chinese characters and pronunciation guide for the terms mentioned in this section.)

DISTRICTS OF BEIJING

Beijing Municipality includes four counties (Huairou, Miyun, Pinggu, and Yanqing), 10 rural districts (Changping, Chaoyang, Daxing, Fangshan, Fengtai, Haidian, Mentougou, Shijingshan, Shunyi, and Tongzhou), and four urban districts (East City, West City, Xuanwu, and Chongwen). The map of Beijing districts on page 30 shows dotted lines that depict the approximate borders of some of these districts. The districts in which most expats live are Haidian and Chaoyang.

Haidian District

In recent years, the Haidian District has become known as the high-tech center of the city. A specific area located in Haidian, called Zhongguancun, is often referred to as China's "Silicon Valley." Traditionally though, the Haidian District has been better known as the location of many of Beijing's finest universities, including Beijing University and Qinghua University, and thus is the home of many foreign teachers and students. (Note: These universities have reverted to using the spellings "Peking University" and "Tsinghua University.")

Chaoyang District

The Chaoyang District has been the most popular home of expats for many years. Their options for housing increased here after the Holiday Inn Lido Beijing opened in the mid-1980s and then built an adjacent compound of apartments. These days, more and more expats—especially those who move to China with small children—are living in "villas," or Western-style detached homes, many of which are located on either side of the highway leading to Beijing Airport.

The Chaoyang District is also the home of the Jianguomenwai and Sanlitun embassy and diplomatic residence compounds; many diplomats live in these neighborhoods, as do many foreign journalists. Both embassies and residence blocks are surrounded by walls, and employ guards to watch every gate. Be forewarned that people who look Asian will generally receive more scrutiny than non-Asians regarding proof of identity and reasons for visiting these compounds. The British Embassy, among

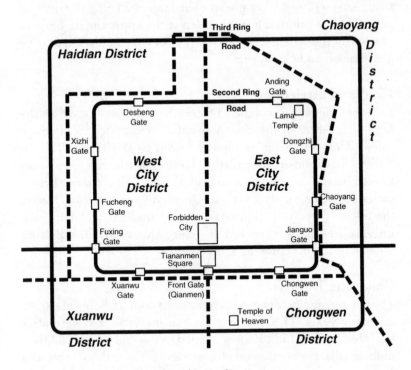

Map of Beijing districts.

others, is located in the Jianguomenwai neighborhood. Embassies such as those of Malaysia and Switzerland are located in Sanlitun. The Japanese Embassy is in the new embassy area just outside the Third Ring Road. Many embassies are outgrowing their traditional locations and planning new buildings, so do confirm the current location of your embassy once you arrive in Beijing.

Other Districts

Relatively less populated by expats are the other four districts of Beijing. The West City District is known for its lakes and parks; Zhongnanhai, the residence of many of the top leaders of China, lies along its eastern edge. The East City District is the home of famous sites such as the Forbidden City and the Lama Temple. The Xuanwu and Chongwen Districts are primarily Chinese residential neighborhoods. Perhaps one could say that the Xuanwu District is the cultural center of Beijing, as it is home to several Chinese opera theaters and Liulichang "Culture Street." The Chongwen District is where the original Beijing Railway Station is situated and is also the site of the Temple of Heaven.

SEASONS AND WEATHER

Whether scheduling activities for your first year in Beijing or suggesting a time for visitors to grace you with their presence, you will probably want to consider what the seasons are like. Fall (September and October) is absolutely the best time of year. The weather is cool and the skies are relatively clear. Winter (November through March) is sometimes depressing due to frigid temperatures and gray skies. Early spring (April and early May) can be windy, kicking up sandstorms that make it uncomfortable to spend time outdoors (see the chapter on *Staying Healthy*). Late May and early June are often quite pleasant. Summer (June through August) can be unbearably hot, but in August occasional night rains cool the temperature to some extent. These distinct

31

seasons can greatly influence the planning of activities by expats living in Beijing.

❊ ❊ ❊

In general, having a feeling for the geography and history of Beijing is a good first step in understanding the local culture and will be an asset as you get to know your new neighbors and colleagues. Use the information you learn about the city to create small talk and build rapport with the Chinese people you meet. They will be delighted that you have made an effort to learn about the history and background of the place they call home.

Funds were diverted from the Chinese navy to build this marble boat, on display at the Summer Palace.

CHAPTER TWO

PEOPLE AND CULTURE

It is helpful to know something about the people of Beijing—also known as "Beijingers"—before you move to the city. Most people consider Beijingers to be people whose families have lived there for at least two generations. They take pride in living in a special place—the capital and political center of China.

PROFILE OF "BEIJINGERS"

Whether outsiders can speak Mandarin or not, they often discover that they can distinguish Beijing people from other Chinese speakers by the ubiquitous "rrrrr" of the local dialect. (This "rrrrr" is like a hard, extended American English "r", as opposed to the trill "r" of Spanish.) People in neighboring Tianjin city have this "rrrrr" in their speech as well, but not to the same extent. While expats say that Beijingers speak like their mouths are full of marbles, Chinese people say that Beijingers speak like they have mouths full of steaming hot *doufu* (bean curd).

Beijingers have other distinctive characteristics as well, such as they don't seem to smile much. This leads outsiders to comment that Beijingers take life too seriously. Many Chinese people think that Beijingers are overly concerned with politics and government policies of the day. Perhaps this is true, but the positive side is that Beijingers are politically savvy; they usually know just how far to bend the rules to get things done without being reprimanded.

Beijingers are generally welcoming hosts who are proud of their capital city and their roles as exemplars of the nation. A certain confidence radiates throughout the city, as though everyone is thinking, "This is where it all starts in China."

CULTURAL PATTERNS

Beijingers share some deep cultural tendencies with other Chinese people. There are plenty of resources from which to learn more about these aspects of culture, so the following observations are simply an introduction:

An orientation toward group activity, rather than individual initiative, is common in Chinese society. Strong networks of relationships—referred to in Mandarin as *guanxi*—are critical to getting things done. Whenever Chinese people must do something that could be difficult or with which they are somewhat unfamiliar, they are likely to think, "Who can help me with this?" rather than "How is it best to accomplish this?" Expats who begin building relationships as soon as they arrive in Beijing can smooth the way for later dealings, especially with bureaucracies.

Awareness of the concept of "face" is critical to understanding the behavior of people in China. "Face" is the appearance of honor and dignity that people have in the eyes of others who know them. Any act or situation that enhances this sense of honor and dignity (such as winning a prestigious award) "gives face." Face is a precious commodity; getting it raises one's status among family, friends, and colleagues. Being given a gift, being treated with respect, and working for a well-known organization all provide face. People also gain face by having strong *guanxi* networks, as they are perceived as having access to vast human resources to get things accomplished. Conversely, a situation that detracts from one's honor and dignity (such as being reprimanded for a mistake) makes a person "lose face." Having a request denied or being singled out for criticism are other occurrences that lead to loss of face. One reason that group effort is preferred over individual initiative in China is that with group effort, the risk of individual loss of face is substantially reduced. Giving face to people you meet in Beijing will smooth the pathways to good, long-term relationships. Making others lose face can damage, and sometimes even end, solid friendships.

Interrelated with "face" is the concept of individual modesty, which is highly valued in Chinese society. Being modest about one's own accomplishments and those of family members gives "face" to others. It is important to respond to compliments with words of denial and to avoid boasting about your spouse or children. (By lowering oneself or one's family, one elevates other people. Despite this rule of thumb, many Chinese parents find it difficult to resist boasting about their children. This is considered a mild faux pas and is usually overlooked or at least tolerated. Often, Chinese parents do not give praise to their children directly, but will brag about them to others.)

Traditional Confucian teachings offered guidelines for behavior when interacting with people one knows, but did not provide much guidance concerning interaction with strangers. Although Confucianism is officially classified as "superstition" in China today, this traditional manner of thinking still has deep implications for modern behavior. If you are a stranger, you matter little to others. Do not take personal offense if someone you don't know bumps into you, for example, and does not offer an apology. Likewise, if you wish to meet someone who is a stranger to you, it is best to have a personal introduction from an intermediary who knows and is respected by both you and the other party. If you make a good impression during the first meeting and can eventually become a *pengyou* (friend), a sense of reciprocity will develop involving mutual obligation to take care of each other.

BEHAVIOR PATTERNS

The people of Beijing also share certain aspects of physical behavior, such as gestures, with other Chinese people. Investigate some of the references listed in the *Resource Guide* and *Further Reading* to learn more about these behavior patterns.

Chinese people will say "yes" or nod their heads to mean a wide variety of things, but most often to mean "I am listening" or "I heard you." Expats who assume that hearing a "yes" or seeing a nod means that Chinese people understand or agree are likely to spend a lot of time feeling disappointed and perhaps feeling deceived. Plan to spend extra time confirming mutual understanding and agreement during your stay in Beijing.

When talking, Chinese people are unlikely to give their conversation partners sustained, direct eye contact. More likely, eye contact will be intermittent and accompanied by "listening sounds," such as "mmm," "ahh," or *dui* (correct). As mentioned earlier, these utterances are simply demonstrations of the act of listening and should not be perceived as expressions of agreement or understanding.

There is a tendency among Chinese people, as well as among other people of East Asia, to smile or laugh when they are nervous or embarrassed. Although laughter in China certainly can signal an appreciative reaction to humor or a pleasant surprise, it would be a mistake to interpret Chinese laughter as having only these meanings. If a Chinese person smiles or laughs after hearing something you have said or seeing something you have done, always consider several possibilities. Perhaps this person considers your words or actions amusing, but perhaps this person feels shame or embarrassment.

Unlike in other East Asian societies, people in China today generally do not bow when greeting others. A nod of the head is all that is necessary to acknowledge another person. In business, handshakes are often accompanied by a nod of the head.

Some gestures that are common among Chinese people are: beckoning to others with all four fingers and with the palm of the hand facing down, demonstrating respect by handing things (such as a gift or a business card) to others with both hands, and pointing to items and people using the entire hand rather than one finger.

FOREIGNERS IN BEIJING

A History: Traders and Invaders

For centuries, the people of China had continuous and extensive contact with a wide array of foreigners including Central Asians, Arabs, Jews, Koreans, Japanese, and non-Han peoples living near China's borders, and occasionally, even with Europeans. Such contacts took place through trade, diplomacy, and warfare. Sometimes, foreigners came to China via land routes such as the Silk Road; other times they came using sea routes. These contacts began as early as the Han Dynasty. During the Tang Dynasty, Beijing was just another town on the northern frontier of the empire, as Chang An (modern Xi'an) was the capital of China and ranked among the most cosmopolitan cities in the world. Until the Yuan Dynasty, for people in Beijing, contact with foreigners was probably limited to interaction with the nomadic tribes near China such as the Khitans and Jurchens, as well as Mongols and Koreans. Unfortunately, foreigners have often brought Beijing residents more turmoil than joy. At first there were the Asian conquerors—the nomads and then, the Mongols and Manchus. Both of these latter two groups discriminated against the Han (Chinese) and prevented them from holding certain positions in government. Later, during the Yuan Dynasty, several people arrived in Beijing from the West. Marco Polo visited then, and during the Ming Dynasty an Italian Jesuit, Matteo Ricci arrived in Beijing. Although Ricci and his Jesuit successors, Johann Adam Schall von Bell and Ferdinand Verbiest (both astronomers), were able to gain the respect of the Chinese imperial courts, ultimately their missionary work had limited impact on Chinese society. However, the propagation of Christian teachings would later fuel popular anti-foreign uprisings.

None of these early encounters with foreigners prepared Beijing's citizens for their encounter with the industrialized world. The relative peace and prosperity of the first half of the Qing Dynasty had produced a fair amount of complacency. In 1793, a British emissary, Lord Macartney, brought a delegation to the Qing court (which was at the time in summer residence north of Beijing) to request that China relax restrictions and tariffs on foreign trade. The Qing emperor eventually refused Macartney's proposal, in essence stating that there was no need to comply with the request as China had no need for foreign wares. Miffed and desperate to balance its trade deficits, Britain began illegally selling opium to private traders in southern China.

Over the next few decades, greater and greater numbers of people in China became addicted to opium. Eventually, a Chinese commissioner enacted measures that virtually eliminated the opium market. Retaliation by the British for that and other acts was termed the "Opium War." China was overpowered and, upon defeat, the Qing court acceded to British demands for opening treaty ports and yielded Hong Kong to British rule under the Treaty of Nanking (1842). Britain did not get the one thing it really coveted, though—representation in Beijing.

A pavilion in the Summer Palace is framed by trees.

In 1858 and 1859, British and French forces threatened China's capital, but never advanced farther than the city of Tianjin. In 1860, however, these forces successfully invaded Beijing and burned the Old Summer Palace in retaliation for the arrest of a British subject and in an effort to intimidate the Qing regime into allowing representation. A convention was signed that year granting Western powers representation in Beijing, and the representatives took up residence in 1861. It should never be forgotten by Western residents in Beijing that their predecessors forced their presence on the city.

Ten years later, in 1871, China had official contact with Japan for the first time in 300 years, but by 1894, they were at war. The conflict lasted less than a year; the treaty signed at the end ceded Taiwan to Japanese rule. During these years, China was unable to protect several tributary states, such as Annam, from the encroachment of Western powers. The loss of territory and threats at its borders made China fear for its existence.

Anti-foreign sentiment rose, and a group called the Boxers began attacking Westerners—mostly missionaries—in 1897. By 1900, they had made their way to Beijing, killing many Chinese

Christians and foreigners and raiding their residences. The Boxers, with the quiet backing of the Qing regime, surrounded the foreign legation in Beijing and held the people inside captive for two months, demanding their expulsion from the city. Seven nations — America, Japan, Austria, Italy, France, Russia, and Britain — banded together and invaded Beijing, forcing the release of the captive foreigners. Germany joined the subsequent negotiations, forcing concessions from the Qing government.

By 1911 when the Qing Dynasty collapsed, much of China's industry and infrastructure was in the hands of foreign powers. The new national government was unable to exercise effective control over the country, and a period of turmoil ensued. While there was much resentment against foreign domination, it also became clear to some Chinese intellectual and political leaders that China needed to modernize by examining and incorporating foreign ideas and institutions — albeit on a decidedly selective basis.

Although Beijing's significance as the political center of China diminished in subsequent years, nonetheless, it was an important center for intellectual debate and political activity. On May 4, 1919, students and others demonstrated in Tiananmen Square to protest China's poor treatment under the Treaty of Versailles, which handed the German-controlled parts of Shandong Province over to Japan at the end of World War I. This demonstration, called the "May Fourth Movement," became the foundation for future movements and new intellectual currents. Many of the ideas behind these movements originated in foreign countries. (The May Fourth Movement was also the forerunner of the socialist movement in China, which led to the formation of the Communist Party in 1921.)

Beijing and much of northeast China came under Japanese occupation from 1937 until 1945. Many people in Beijing deeply resented — and some still resent — this time of domination. During the 30 years from 1949–1979, foreigners were virtually locked out of Beijing, although China had visits from and close contact with Russians and North Koreans. China also accepted communists expelled from countries such as Singapore and the Philippines, many of whom still live in Beijing today.

The Later Years

Since 1979, the influx of foreigners and other outsiders to Beijing has grown dramatically. Due to resumption of the examination system for acceptance into higher-level institutions of learning, its universities attract the best and brightest students from all over China. Students also go to Beijing from a variety of other countries; some to study Mandarin and others to pursue studies in specific fields or industries. Diplomats and journalists also arrive from all over the world to live and work in this major world capital and the center of government of all of China. Businesspeople flock to China in pursuit of the world's largest consumer market, establishing offices in Beijing to function as their headquarters. It is this environment that awaits expats today.

By the way, it is important to clarify one point concerning foreigners; more specifically, white foreigners. Many have the notion that when local people speak about them in Mandarin, they use all kinds of awful names that include the words "devil" or "barbarian." This might be true to some extent in southern China, but generally not in Beijing. If Chinese people know that you speak Mandarin, they might refer to you as a *waibin* or "foreign guest." If you don't speak Mandarin, they might call you a *dabizi* or "big nose," which refers to the fact that most white people's noses protrude quite prominently from their faces instead of lying flat against the face. In any case, the term "big nose" is generally used in a friendly rather than a derogatory way. The third and most common term used to refer to all foreigners, is *laowai* or "old outsider." This is a fairly neutral term, in which "old" is used in the sense of "good old" rather than in direct reference to age.

41

According to the Confucian classic *The Analects*, "To have friends visit from distant places, isn't it joyous!" Chinese people are ethically bound to be hospitable to visitors. Most estimates concur that Beijing today is home to more than 100,000 people from other countries, and some estimates that include people from China's territories put the figure at about 200,000 expats living in the city. These expats are teachers and students, diplomats and other embassy employees, technical experts, journalists, business executives, and all their families. They hail from every corner of the world and make the foreign community of Beijing rich in diversity. Living in the midst of such diversity is one of the most stimulating aspects of making one's home in the capital of China.

MAKING GOOD IMPRESSIONS

In Beijing, it is especially important to make a good impression when you first meet with local people. Your initial actions will strongly influence their desire to associate with you and their willingness to help you when you need assistance. According to Chinese thinking, the type of person you are is as important as— or even more important than—whatever you are trying to accomplish. Observe the following guidelines whether you're meeting for the first time your new boss, a rental agent, the head of the department at the university, or people you will be managing.

The impression you convey to people in Beijing is based largely on how "civilized" you are, which includes how you speak and act (politely and modestly), how you dress (nicely to give face, but not ostentatiously), how well you observe rules of protocol and etiquette (acting as a guest when you are a guest and acting as a host when you are a host), and even the topics of conversation you choose. Another important component of making a good impression on people is your ability to make a "connection" or establish common ground with them. This common ground could be something similar in your backgrounds or some area of mutual interest. For people of Chinese heritage, the impression you make on others could be based on how well you speak Mandarin.

Of course, the behavior of Chinese people described in this chapter and in other parts of this book can vary widely. The behavior of people you meet could be different depending on what part of China they are originally from, how much exposure they have to Westerners and other expats, and how close your relationships are with them. Another factor is age. Young people are likely to be influenced by behavior that they see in foreign television programs and movies, and may want to adapt to your style. Take your cue from the people you meet as to the best ways to interact with them.

DRESS

It is generally a good idea to dress well for first meetings. As a sign of respect, err on the side of formality. Jeans would be inappropriate, but nice trousers and a jacket would be acceptable for both men and women. Flashy attire and excessive jewelry are rarely appropriate in Beijing. After an initial meeting, as you become more familiar with each other, it is fine to dress less formally. In this regard, follow the lead of your hosts in Beijing to gauge how you should dress. Naturally, on important occasions such as formal banquets, people will dress more formally, but never to the extent of "black tie" lavishness. (This doesn't mean that you should leave your black-tie garb at home, though. Various expat groups organize a few black-tie events each year.)

Most colors can be seen adorning the modern fashions of Beijing. Traditionally, red has been considered a festive color, and it is often used in children's clothing. Although Chinese people traditionally dressed completely in white only when participating in mourning rituals, many young women ignore this tradition and wear all-white outfits. Generally, only young people are seen dressed all in black, as it is also considered a color of mourning.

Chinese men and women rarely wear shorts or sleeveless shirts in professional settings. However, many people wear this type of casual attire at home or during weekend activities in Beijing. (Western men with hairy legs quickly switch to wearing only long pants when traveling in rural areas, as small children sometimes pull on their leg hair.) Women virtually never wear clothing that exposes their midriffs.

ETIQUETTE

Chinese etiquette is guided by a host/guest hierarchy. If you travel to Beijing only for short visits, you will almost always find yourself in the role of the guest. Once you move to Beijing, however, people will expect you to be more savvy about the nuances of local culture—for example, knowing who should play the role of host and who should play the role of guest in any given situation, and knowing how to behave accordingly. Usually the determination of roles is influenced by one or more of the following factors: who is oldest; in whose territory the meeting is taking place; if a meal is involved, who is paying the bill, and perhaps even who suggested having the meal in the first place.

Generally speaking, hosts show hospitality by demonstrating concern for and taking care of guests. A good host never leaves guests standing and instead insists that they sit down. Whenever possible, a good Chinese host always begins discussions by offering guests a cup of tea. (If a Chinese person visits your home or office, no matter how well you know the person or how rushed you feel, never forget this little formality.) Guests should respond by saying, "Oh, no, it's too much trouble." The host will insist and the guests then accept and express appreciation and gratitude for the hospitality—even if they have been drinking tea all day and do not plan to take more than one symbolic sip.

CONVERSATION TOPICS

At the beginning of a relationship, Chinese people often use questions to simultaneously demonstrate modesty (by diverting attention from themselves) and search for areas of common interest. Ask people in Beijing if they are originally from that city or from some other place in China, as Chinese people take great pride in their hometown or region and its culture. Ask them which part of the city they live in. Ask them if they've ever had a chance to visit your country.

On the other hand, it's not a good idea to ask people how many children they have, as China's one-child policy is quite strictly enforced in Beijing. Instead, ask, "How many people are there in your family?" (Many Chinese people live with extended family such as a grandparent or an aunt.) Don't ask people to make restaurant recommendations as they might take this as a hint that you want them to invite you to dinner. Avoid questions concerning people's opinions on domestic politics and international affairs, including the issue of Taiwan, until you know them exceptionally well, and even then it is best to ask in private.

As for other topics of conversation, please don't discuss the weather or your pets. Instead, talk about favorable impressions of Beijing. Tell people what historic sites you've visited recently. Discuss the Olympics. Food is always a favorite topic—prepare yourself by reading the chapter on *The Chinese Dining Experience*.

❊ ❊ ❊

In general, making a good impression on your hosts should greatly smooth your way in Beijing. By remembering to conduct yourself as a gracious visitor and by making a serious effort to adapt to local customs, you can begin to build relationships that just might last a lifetime.

— CHAPTER THREE —

CHINESE LANGUAGE

It is said that there are seven or eight mutually unintelligible dialects of Chinese, and Mandarin is one of them. It is by far the best dialect for foreigners to study, because over 70% of China's population speaks Mandarin as a native dialect. Among the other dialects of spoken Chinese are Cantonese (spoken by people in Hong Kong and certain parts of Guangdong Province) and Minnan (spoken in southern Fujian Province).

Technically, the dialect of Beijing is derived from the "standard Mandarin" dialect. Some Beijingers have the ability to switch to standard Mandarin at will—especially when talking with speakers of other dialects—and when they do, they generally speak clear, beautiful Mandarin. An interesting finding of one survey was that almost 30% of native Beijingers could not distinguish between the Beijing dialect and standard Mandarin. The higher the level of education among those surveyed, though, the greater the likelihood that they could make distinctions with respect to pronunciation and vocabulary.

SPOKEN AND WRITTEN FORMS

In this book, for the sake of familiarity and convenience, we refer collectively to the standard dialect of Chinese and the spoken language of Beijing as "Mandarin." When we refer to all dialects of spoken Chinese, we use the terms "Chinese" or "Chinese language." In China, the official term for the standard Mandarin dialect is *putonghua* (common speech). Other terms used colloquially and their literal translations include *zhongwen* (center language), *zhongguo hua* (center country speech), *hanyu* (Han tongue), and *guoyu* (country tongue). The Chinese equivalent of "Mandarin" — *guanhua* (officials' speech) — is virtually never used among Chinese people.

The formal written language used by speakers of Mandarin and all other dialects is composed of Chinese characters. These characters, which are basically ideographs (each character contains an idea or concept), could each be pronounced in many different ways depending on the dialects of the people reading them. The structure and vocabulary of the formal written language most closely match those of Mandarin. When reference is made to the written Chinese language, usually we use the terms "Chinese" or "Chinese characters."

Characters come in two forms: traditional and simplified. People who are of Chinese descent and who live outside China, as well as those who live in Chinese territories, are generally most familiar with the traditional forms of the characters. In the 1950s, the government of China authorized simplified versions of some characters. The vocabulary lists in the *Glossary* include both "simplified" and "traditional" Chinese characters for the reference of all our readers.

INTRODUCTION TO MANDARIN

If you have not already arranged to take Mandarin lessons, the brief introduction offered here will help you get started. Those who are just beginning to take lessons might find this overview useful as a supplement.

All Chinese dialects are tonal—the meanings of words change when speakers change the tones in which the words are pronounced. In Mandarin, there are (only!) four tones. Thus, using the syllable "ma" as an example, when it is pronounced in the first tone it means "mother"; pronounced in the second tone it means "hemp" (a type of grass that is used to make rope); pronounced in the third tone it means "horse"; and pronounced in the fourth tone it means "to scold." The chart below is a graphic illustration of these tones. Think of the dotted line as your normal tone of speech.

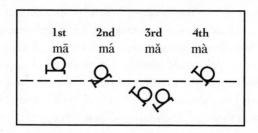

The four tones of Mandarin Chinese.

To describe this in another way using English equivalents, the first tone is pronounced like the word "I" in the phrase, "I see" The second tone (also called the "rising tone") is pronounced like the exclamation, "What?" The third tone is pronounced like "Well", when used to mean "What do you have to say for yourself?" The fourth tone (also called the "falling tone") is pronounced like the casual greeting, "Hi!"

The typical Chinese word order is, very generally speaking, similar to that of English: subject-verb-object. With few exceptions, there is no difference between singular and plural nouns. For example, *Ta you shu* can mean either, "He has a book" or "He has books." (An exception is that nouns and pronouns that refer to humans can be made plural by adding the suffix–*men*. Thus the common greeting *Ni hao ma?* or "How are you?" can be stated *Nimen hao ma?* when greeting a group of people rather than an individual.)

There are limited ways to express time with verbs in Chinese, so speakers usually use some other word to indicate time (*Wo qu* can mean both "I go" and "I will go." A word such as "tomorrow" must be added in order to clearly differentiate between present and future. More advanced speakers of Mandarin know that sometimes the word *yao* is used to indicate the future, but it is unreliable as a future indicator because it also can mean "to want" Thus *Wo yao qu* can mean either "I want to go" or "I will go," or both, depending on the context.)

The good news is that Chinese has no articles (such as "a" and "the" in English, or "la" and "les" in French). See how easy it will be to learn to speak Mandarin?

LEARNING MANDARIN

Before moving to Beijing, many people who cannot speak Mandarin ask, "Should I try to learn some Mandarin? Won't people in Beijing be upset if I mangle their language?" Generally speaking, the answers to the questions are "Yes" and "No," respectively. A little language goes a long way toward making your stay more comfortable, while demonstrating your interest in the local people and culture. It is extremely rare to hear of a

Chinese person becoming upset or angry by a foreigner's attempt to speak Mandarin. As a matter of fact, asking local people to help you with pronunciation or with some other aspect of the language is likely to build an incredible amount of goodwill. It also gives you something to talk about when you're tired of talking about food.

Of course, there are plenty of foreigners living happily in Beijing who have little ability in spoken Mandarin, and even more who have no ability in reading Chinese characters. Some newly arrived foreigners who cannot read Chinese comment, with frustration, that they have never before known what it is like to be illiterate. Foreigners who cannot speak Mandarin or read Chinese characters sometimes feel isolated from daily life in Beijing and restricted to staying within the expat community.

How best to manage the process of learning the local language is often a primary concern for people moving to foreign countries. Adults have good reason to be concerned, as the amount of time and effort it takes to learn a foreign language increases with age. Children, however, learn languages quickly. One family that moved to Beijing had a daughter who was eight years old. As there was no slot immediately available for her in the English-speaking international schools, the family enrolled her in a French school. On a daily basis, she spoke English with her family members, French in school, and Mandarin outside the home and with the housekeeper. Like most young children who are exposed to more than one language, she had little problem keeping the languages separate and functioned quite effectively in all of them.

Private Tutors

Adults who move to Beijing and want to learn Chinese can pursue one or more of several options. The first and most expensive option is to hire a private tutor — although the word "expensive" is relative. (People from Japan, for example, would probably find the cost of a private tutor in Beijing quite reasonable.) For those who go the tutor route, it is strongly suggested that you designate a trial period with the new tutor. It is acceptable to end your sessions with the tutor at the end of the trial period if you do not feel comfortable or if you feel that you are not making progress. Many people try two or three tutors before finding one who uses teaching methods that match their learning styles.

Courses

Other options include attending classes that concentrate on developing basic speaking and listening abilities for small groups of adult foreigners, or attending somewhat rigorous university programs that are designed for younger students and usually include an emphasis on reading and writing Chinese characters.

Immersion courses are a great way to get started in your language-learning efforts, if you can afford the up-front investment of at least one week. Several of these are available in Beijing, although many are offered at sites in the Haidian District, far from the residences and offices of most expats, because of better access to university professors.

Timing

When considering the timing of your language sessions, remember that mornings are best—it is easiest to comprehend and retain new things when your brain is fresh. Adults require more regular repetition and reinforcement than do children, so the frequency of sessions is more important than the length. For example, a business executive is likely to progress faster by having a tutor come to the office for 45-minute sessions three days per week, than by attending a three-hour evening class once a week.

Several, but not all, options for learning Mandarin in Beijing have been explored here. It is important to keep in mind that these are simply suggestions. Learning a new language is an intensely personal experience. People learn languages in different ways and at different speeds. Be patient and persistent until you figure out which methods work best for you.

TIPS FOR CHINESE SPEAKERS

While Beijingers can usually tell who is local and who is not by hairstyles, clothing, shoes, and especially speech, they often automatically expect foreigners who look Asian to be able to speak some dialect of Chinese. If you look Asian and are not Chinese, and if you can find a way to communicate to Beijing residents which country you are from or which language you speak, they are likely to be understanding and accommodating. On the other hand, if you look Asian and are of Chinese heritage, then you will find that Beijingers have high expectations concerning your use of Mandarin. You are expected to either blend in and speak it perfectly or else endure a certain degree of prejudice and ostracism. In other words, people who speak Cantonese or another Chinese dialect—as well as non-Chinese students who studied in Taiwan— should get some training in the pronunciation, grammar, and vocabulary of standard Mandarin either before or when they move to Beijing. As for people who are of Chinese heritage and say they can't speak Mandarin at all...well, Beijingers just won't believe them.

Here are some "blending in" guidelines for people of Chinese heritage who do not speak standard Mandarin as their native dialect. By devoting time and effort to developing skills in these areas, you can make a positive impression on people you meet in Beijing. Find a tutor who can help you with the following:

1. Memorize proper pronunciations in order to diminish the frequency with which you must guess the pronunciation of words.

2. Learn and always enunciate the difference in pronunciation among/between words such as:

- 基 jī, 折 zhē, 之 zhī, and 咨 zī
- 奢 shē, 失 shī, and 私 sī
- 宗 zōng, 葱 cōng, and 充 chōng
- 酥 sū and 输 shū
- 粗 cū and 出 chū

3. People who tend to intermittently use English words when speaking Chinese, as many people do in Hong Kong and Singapore, absolutely must learn and use Chinese equivalents. In Beijing, even people who speak English well rarely mix Chinese and English.

4. The vowel sounds used by speakers of northern or standard Mandarin are generally longer or more "stretched out" than those used by speakers of southern Chinese dialects. This makes Mandarin sound "fluid" rather than "staccato." Do your best to imitate these longer vowel sounds when speaking Mandarin.

5. Northern speakers of Mandarin use far fewer particles at the end of their sentences and these particles are also noticeably different. For example, they rarely end sentences with the particle "ah" as speakers of some southern Chinese dialects do. Pay attention to the particles used by people in Beijing and modify your speech accordingly.

6. Questions that are constructed verb + negative + verb (such as *"Hao bu hao?"* or *"You mei you?"*) can seem condescending to Beijingers, as they generally use the verb + *ma* construction (*"Hao ma?"* or *"Hou ma?"*). In certain instances, though (for example, when a shopper wishes to convey extreme frustration to a shop clerk), the verb + negative + verb construction is sometimes used.

CHINESE NAMES

The best way to begin language- (or dialect-) learning efforts, and a way to consistently make a good impression on your new colleagues, friends, and neighbors in Beijing, is to work hard at pronouncing and using Chinese family names (surnames) correctly. The most awful pronunciation mistake is made by native speakers of English who often say the Chinese name Wang by pronouncing the "a" as the **a** in apple. Use the **a** in father instead. When you don't, it makes the little hairs on the backs of people's necks stand on end.

In order to pronounce and use Chinese family names, you must first learn to distinguish them from given names. Unfortunately, this is sometimes impossible to do if you cannot read Chinese characters, because in Mandarin there are so many homonyms (words having the same pronunciation). The best course of action is to clarify with people when you meet them which name is the family name. Being familiar with some of the more common Chinese family names can also be helpful. A few of these are listed in the *Glossary*.

As for the order of Chinese names, the family name comes first and is usually just one syllable; the family name is followed by a one- or two-character given name.

Example:
Liu Daming (Liu is the one-syllable family name or surname.)

Exception:
Sima Jun (Sima is one of the rare two-syllable family names. This person has only a one-character given name.)

In the example above, there is no space between the syllables *Da* and *ming* in the given name. This is the proper way to indicate a given name, but many Chinese people do not know this. After all, among themselves they use Chinese characters, not Roman letters, to write their names. A good rule of thumb is that 98% of the time, when you see two syllables printed together, this is the given name. (Chinese people from some places around the world connect the two syllables of the given name using a hyphen, but this method is rarely used in China today.)

Chinese people sometimes alter the word order of their names for the benefit of Westerners. If there is any question in your mind as to which is the family name, ask the person to clarify. One clue as to which is the given name, as was mentioned earlier, might be that two syllables are joined together.

Example:
Daming Liu (This person has reversed the order of his name and surname to "help" Westerners who don't speak Mandarin identify his surname.)

Sometimes Chinese people who work for foreign companies choose Western given names, such as "Pierre" or "Lucy." This is convenient for foreigners, making it easy to distinguish the family name and easy to pronounce the given name. However, for official purposes and among themselves, Chinese people generally continue to use their Chinese names.

It's a good idea for non-Chinese expats to have Chinese names, as these names are easier for local people to pronounce and remember. Ask a language teacher or some other friendly, knowledgeable Chinese person to help you choose an appropriate name containing some of the sounds or meaning of your original name. As your Mandarin improves during your stay, Beijingers are likely to begin using your Chinese name exclusively. This should be taken as a compliment!

Occasionally, when choosing a Chinese name for you, people will suggest a transliterated name. This, however, should be resisted, as the more syllables in your original name, the more awkward it gets from the Chinese point of view. The French name Odile Perrin, for example, might be transliterated as *Ou-di-le/Pi-rang*. Therefore, in choosing a Chinese name, it is a good idea to adhere to the pattern of a one- or two-character family name followed by a one- or two-syllable given name.

In case you were wondering, there is really no way to distinguish between male and female given names unless one can read Chinese characters, and even then it is sometimes difficult.

FORMS OF ADDRESS

If you know the official title of a person you meet, it is important to use that title when addressing the person. ("Very nice to see you again, Manager Li.") However, if you do not know a person's formal title, there are several other forms of address that you can use. Note that in Chinese the family names come before these forms of address. Those most commonly used are:

mister (Mr.) = *xiansheng*
Example: Mr. Liu = Liu *xiansheng*

miss = *xiaojie*
Example: Miss Ma = Ma *xiaojie*

madame (Mme.) = *nüshi*
Example: Madame Jin = Jin *nüshi*

The latter title, "Madame" (or *nüshi* in Mandarin), is the preferred form of address in China today for older and/or married women. Although some speakers of Mandarin use the term *taitai*, meaning "Mrs.," expats should use neither *taitai* nor "Mrs." until they are more familiar with the people and customs of Beijing.

Typically used with the husband's family name, *taitai* could be translated as "wife of." Women in China rarely take the family names of their husbands when they marry, and it is inappropriate to use this term unless you know the husband very well.

Incidentally, to refer to a spouse of either gender, people in Beijing and many other areas of China use the generic term *airen*, which literally means "lover." (Please note: If you are a native speaker of another dialect of Chinese, using *airen* in this manner may seem awkward to you at first. Do not feel self-conscious when using this term. It is important to blend in and follow local customs in your new home.) However, some young Chinese people in Beijing find it fashionable to use *taitai* for the term "wife" instead of *airen*. Other terms used to refer to wives are *furen* (formal) and *laopo* (informal).

If Chinese people you meet have chosen Western given names such as "Pierre" or "Lucy," it is usually acceptable to refer to them by those names. Otherwise, use their Chinese family names along with appropriate titles. With people who are about your age, it is acceptable to use their Chinese given names together with their family names. (For example, when greeting a colleague whom you have not seen in a couple of weeks, you could say, "Hey! Liu Daming! How are you doing?") In Chinese society, younger people rarely call older people by their given names. Instead, they might use the term *lao* (old) plus the older person's family name.

To get a stranger's attention, in English, people often loudly say, "Miss!" or "Mister!" or "Sir!" In Mandarin, it is acceptable to call the attention of young women by using *xiaojie* (Miss), but the other common titles are generally not used to get someone's attention. A few Chinese people still use *tongzhi* (comrade) for a generic way of calling out to a worker, such as a shop clerk; however, it would be inappropriate for expats to imitate this custom. Another term is *shifu* (master worker), although this is generally reserved for older, male workers. The best ways to approach anyone you don't know are to say, *Qing wen...*, which means "Please may I ask...", or *Mafan ni...*, which translated, loosely means "May I bother you...," and then pause until you have that person's attention.

* * *

As a footnote to the introduction of language issues, some foreigners ask why the name of Beijing was changed from "Peking". Actually, the name never changed—the characters were pronounced "Beijing" in the standard Mandarin dialect even when the spelling "Peking" was used among foreigners. Most historians and linguists say that the spelling "Peking" was based on the Cantonese pronunciation of the Chinese characters, because much early news about China was recounted to people abroad by foreigners living in or visiting southern China. Using an old phonetic system that used a "p" to spell the sound "b", and a "k" to spell the sound "g", the Cantonese pronunciation was spelled "Peking." A more useful rendering might be "bahk-ging."

Learning the nuances of the spoken language in your new home can be revealing, fun, and rewarding. Although you might struggle to learn this new language, your efforts will be worth the trouble. If you can learn to recognize a few Chinese characters as well, it will alleviate feelings of illiteracy and help you get around in the city. Relax and be confident, knowing that many people have already gone through this process before you and have eventually thrived.

— Chapter Four —

FINDING A HOME

Residing in a dwelling in which you (and your family members if they are joining you) feel "at home" is an essential component of having a positive experience living in Beijing. It is important to select not only a neighborhood but also a residence that will best suit you in terms of needs and lifestyle. Beijing offers three distinct types of neighborhoods—urban, suburban, and rural. In order to lay a solid foundation for the months ahead, there are several factors to consider in making your decision.

URBAN HOUSING

In spite of efforts to modernize, Beijing's highways, buses, and subway struggle to keep pace with increasing loads of human and vehicular traffic. Proximity to work and schools is therefore becoming increasingly precious. Urban housing (within or just outside the Third Ring Road) is by far the most popular choice for expats living in Beijing, as it offers not only physical proximity to popular destinations, but also provides access to multiple transportation options. Expats who do not drive appreciate the convenience and independence offered by mass transit and a ready supply of taxis (see the chapter on *Getting Around Beijing*).

There are other matters to consider as well. One is medical care, and the finest facilities in Beijing are located primarily in the urban setting. This could be important for families with very small children or with a chronically ill family member, as they may need more than occasional medical attention. Another matter to consider is the availability of goods and services. Urban areas offer shops selling imported goods, as well as convenient access to business services such as professional photocopying and computer repair.

On the downside, air and noise pollution are part and parcel of urban living. Early morning noise is common throughout Chinese society but especially in urban areas, as people seem to begin their daily activities as soon as they are awake. Otherwise, Beijing is relatively quiet. Sirens and car alarms are heard less frequently than in other cities around the world.

For expats who would like to have more contact with Chinese people than with other expats, the urban setting is probably the best. Some of the high-rise buildings constructed specifically to house expats are now permitted to admit local residents as well, but there are smaller apartment buildings around the city that will bring you even closer to Chinese daily life. From these smaller buildings, you might be able to hear the goings-on in a local market or work unit, or you might get glimpses of life in courtyard homes as you move about the neighborhood. This setting is in sharp contrast with the neighborhood surrounding the apartments at the China World Trade complex, for example, which includes mostly foreign-invested hotels and commercial enterprises. The issues that might arise from living in more "local" surroundings, especially in these smaller buildings with as few as six apartment units, will vary depending on which culture you are from originally and the type of living environment to which you are accustomed.

Some expats feel that living in closer contact with the local community offers little privacy, and that living in a small building that houses expats offers virtually none. The neighbors and local vendors will talk about you and want to get to know you, but depending on their level of fluency in English might hesitate to converse much with you if they know that you don't speak Mandarin. Because every apartment building has some kind of security, your entrances and exits will be duly watched and noted—and the fewer residents to keep track of, the more easily your activities will be remembered.

These facilities are also sometimes maintained according to local standards rather than to international ones. For example, the heat might not be turned on until November 15 each year (the date for local facilities), rather than October 15 (the date for most buildings that receive or house expats and foreign guests). Likewise, the heat might be turned off in March rather than April. Or, the elevator—if there is one—might be turned off at 11 p.m. and might not get turned on again until 6 a.m.

Living closer to the local culture has its benefits, though. Expats who truly desire to improve their Mandarin can practice on a daily basis; the language swirls around them each time they enter the neighborhood. Also, this environment can help expats keep local standards of living and consumer habits in perspective; those who work for foreign multinational corporations sometimes have a rather skewed view of the domestic consumer market.

61

Overall, a local living experience will remind you every day that you are indeed in Beijing, which is something you can forget when you are sitting in an apartment in the China World Trade complex, in the lobby of a five-star hotel, or in a well-appointed downtown office.

SUBURBAN HOUSING

Not every expat works in a downtown office building, and those who work in the suburbs of Beijing—perhaps teaching at a university in the outer part of Haidian district or working in a manufacturing facility south of the city—might find a suburban neighborhood more convenient. Expats with children over the age of four or five also frequently choose this option, in order to take advantage of the amenities offered by villas. Families that enjoy outdoor activities on the weekends will find access easier from suburban housing.

A drawback to the suburban setting is the relatively limited access to transportation to the downtown area. Only a few shopping facilities and local produce markets are within walking distance of homes in most suburban housing complexes. Many complexes have shuttle buses to take children to the international schools, but not all schools are consistently served. (They generally require a minimum of four children per complex before providing bus service.) Children who participate in after-hours, extra-curricular activities must sometimes be picked up from school by car, whether a taxi or company vehicle. Suburban complexes often provide shuttle buses to the downtown area (usually running once every 30 minutes during daytime hours), but most of these buses do not run in the very early morning or late evening. Either private drivers or taxis must be hired to supplement the schedule of shuttle buses, and this can get expensive.

Another drawback is that expats might feel isolated and, unless an *ayi*(domestic helper) visits every day, could exist in a foreign cocoon for extended periods, rarely if ever seeing a Chinese person or hearing any Mandarin. Some people who have never lived outside their home countries actually appreciate this environment, as the residents of multiple nationalities offer exposure to a variety of cultures without the shock of more intense immersion in the ocean of Chinese society. On the other hand, expats who are quite shy or who are not adventurous might find that this relatively isolated environment reinforces their own natural tendencies.

RURAL HOUSING

Rural housing, such as the Woodland Villas complex, is basically suburban housing taken to an extreme. Homes are detached, single-family residences clustered in gated communities well outside the Fourth Ring Road. Trips downtown from these complexes take at least one-and-a-half hours. Expats who have previously lived in rural communities in their home countries or who already have an established network of friends in Beijing might be able to thrive in this type of housing, but it is not recommended for most other newcomers.

SELECTING AN AGENT

After deciding on the type of neighborhood in which you want to live, the next step is to visit as many homes and as many types of homes as possible. The most efficient way to do this is to have the assistance of a rental agent. If your company or organization does not designate an agent for you, the best way to find one is to ask other expats or local Chinese contacts for referrals.

It also might be possible to get referrals prior to your departure for Beijing. Find out if anyone in your community has lived in Beijing; search online bulletin boards; ask other people in your organization if they can make recommendations. Once you find one or two agents, use email to contact them and tell them about yourself and your family, along with your expectations concerning housing. You will save yourself and the agents time if you list your requirements in order of priority. Ask potential agents if any fees will be charged for their services. (If a rental professional asks you to pay a small fee for each home or apartment you visit, discontinue working with this person. There should be no fees payable until a housing contract is signed, and at that time the fees are usually paid by the "landlord.")

After narrowing your selection down to a couple of candidates, talk with them at least once via telephone before leaving for Beijing. Casually ask where they are originally from in China; agents who are Beijingers are your best bet, as they are most likely to be familiar with all of the neighborhoods in the city. Also inquire about their experience working with expats. While there are many self-proclaimed real estate experts in Beijing whose contacts with one or two relevant Chinese officials can facilitate the completion of paperwork involved in renting a place to live, many of them are inexperienced at understanding the housing expectations of expats from various parts of the world.

SELECTING A RESIDENCE

In China, almost all land is owned by the government. Even companies building manufacturing plants in China can obtain only land-use rights. When you hear of apartments or other housing units "for sale," this means that the rights to use those facilities for a specific number of years, as opposed to stakes in the real property for perpetuity, are being sold. The government has not been as fast about turning Beijing apartments into "sale units" as it has in some other cities; in other words, the government has retained control of many housing units, which are then available for rent or allocated to Chinese families by the authorities. Certain buildings and housing units are designated by the government as available for use by expats. Some long-term expats in Beijing have "purchased" their homes, but most expats rent their homes, whether those homes are apartments or villas.

In certain cases, expats "purchase" homes and then rent them out to other expats. If the expats who "own" the homes do not live in Beijing, they might designate a local person to manage the process of renting out the home. In these cases, the absentee expats and the people designated as managers are collectively referred to as "landlords." Choose among "landlords" wisely. Their responsiveness to problems and ability to fix them to the satisfaction of expat renters can vary greatly.

There are basically three types of housing available in Beijing, particularly in the urban areas: apartment complexes, villas (or townhomes), and traditional Chinese courtyard homes. Of course, some expats will find their search for suitable housing limited by what they can afford and by the status that they want to convey through their selection. Visiting foreign scholars, for example, might share housing or live in housing provided by the hosting university, as their salaries might not cover even the medium-priced housing that is on the market. The president of the China operations of a multinational company, however, for reasons of status, should probably live either in a suburban villa or in a nicely appointed penthouse apartment downtown.

Apartments

Apartment buildings or complexes of buildings where expats are permitted to live are located primarily in the Chaoyang District, with a few in the East City, Haidian, and Chongwen Districts. Most offer just the basics: 24-hour hot water and elevator service. Others, particularly when annexed to hotel complexes such as the Swissôtel or the Holiday Inn Lido, offer access to fitness facilities, but renters must sometimes pay additional fees to enjoy this privilege.

Most single people working in Beijing choose to live in apartments in the Chaoyang and East City Districts. If you are single and plan to share a local standard apartment, you could pay as little as US$500 per month in rent. It is a good idea to budget more, however, if you do not plan to share an apartment; expect to pay at least US$1,800 per month for a two-bedroom unit that provides most of the amenities preferred by expats. Larger apartments that can accommodate families will be more expensive. Fancy apartments, such as penthouse units, are the most costly.

Villas

Villas are detached housing units, usually offering at least three bedrooms, a garage, a small front yard, and a slightly larger

Tall office and apartment buildings can be seen from the Summer Palace.

backyard. Some villa complexes also have fitness facilities available for residents. Despite their out-of-the-way location and because of the amenities and atmosphere they offer, these units can be pricey, often costing more than US$8,000 in rent per month. Although primarily rented to expats, these days, a few families representative of Beijing's nouveau riche also live in villas.

Courtyard Homes

Sometimes referred to in English as "quadrangles," old courtyard-style homes or *siheyuan* are mostly found in the West and East City Districts. Once the homes of the governmental and commercial elite, they now usually house several local families simultaneously. Most *siheyuan* (and some local apartment buildings as well) cannot legally be rented to expats, so if an agent suggests such a residence, approach the offer with extreme caution. There are plenty of stories about foreigners being encouraged to rent housing units where they cannot legally live; unfortunately, the first inkling they have that their housing situation is not legal might be a visit from local security or housing officials. For those who can read Chinese, one way to determine whether a unit is legal for foreigners to rent is to ask the rental agent or "landlord" to show you a copy of the certificate of ownership.

Prices for courtyard homes can vary widely, depending on several factors: the neighborhood in which they are located, whether or not they are legal for foreigners to rent, and whether or not they provide facilities that meet modern standards (such as indoor plumbing). Expats who are interested in renting one of these homes would be wise to find another alternative for at least their first year in Beijing while they do some research on living in courtyard-style homes.

Housing Issues

For a variety of reasons, taxes can be an issue for renters in Beijing.

Obtain a tax receipt for all housing rental payments in order to exclude rental costs from your taxable income in China, and to protect yourself in case the "landlord" is evading payment of taxes.

A different issue, but one that arises again and again among expats living in villas and newer apartment buildings, is the questionable quality of building materials, fixtures, and craftsmanship, despite outrageous prices. One explanation is that builders commonly lack training and experience, as well as access to quality materials at the precise moment when the materials are needed. In China, with its tremendously large population, there is intense pressure on rather limited resources. This, among other factors, leads to a tendency among Chinese people to work hard to make the best of the resources available at any given time and in any given situation. Results that are *cha bu ∂uo* (meaning "close enough"; literally, "difference not great") are usually considered adequate.

When viewed from a distance, villas and newer apartment buildings can appear very Western and modern. Up close, however, flaws can be glaring. For example, a rental agent boasted that one of the brand new villas near the airport had a lovely marble countertop in the bathroom. Upon closer inspection it was evident that only the top of the marble slab had been polished. The front and sides were dull stone.

Insist on visiting in person any unit that you will rent to determine if you can live with its flaws. Often, the flaws are impossible to remedy, or fixing them might require more patience, money, time, and effort than you could ever imagine. Don't expect to find a unit that has no flaws. Initially you might be appalled at the overall lack of quality materials and workmanship in the units you see, but after you have seen several, you may become more familiar with local standards and decide that you can live with certain compromises. Some expats just do their best to approach the situation with a sense of humor: an advertisement posted by a renter looking for a roommate read, "Everything is super nice (everything works)."

CONFIRMING DETAILS

Here is a basic list of questions to ask and items of which to make note when investigating any housing option:

- Confirm independently, either by talking to expats or by perusing lists of housing for expats, that the unit is officially designated to house foreigners. (Lists of housing are available from *Xianzai Beijing* and many other sources. Please refer to the *Resource Guide* for more information. However, housing units listed in these resources are not guaranteed to be legal for foreigners to rent or buy.)
- What kind of television transmission is available? This can range from local Chinese-language stations only to 24-hour international cable TV access.
- What hours do the elevators run? In some buildings, a couple of self-service elevators run 24 hours per day. In other buildings, a single elevator might be staffed with an operator and only run from about 6 a.m. to 11 p.m.
- What about water and plumbing? Many Chinese courtyard homes, for example, do not have indoor plumbing or toilets. In apartment buildings, find out where the hot water comes from. If hot water comes from a small, individual heating unit rather than from a central one, bear in mind that the water pressure often must be kept low in order for the unit to function, and that gas tanks must be obtained and then replenished when the contents are depleted.
- What about electricity? Who pays for access? Do blackouts occur? Short blackouts occur often in some neighborhoods, particularly at night. The circuit breakers in some older facilities might buckle under typical expat usage, which can

be quite heavy. Toaster ovens, microwaves, air condition-
ers   and pace heaters are often culprits of overload. Be sure to
ask current residents about these issues.

- Test everything. Do toilets flush properly? Do light switches
work? If not, ask to have these items fixed before signing a
contract. Do not accept promises that malfunctioning items
will be fixed after you have signed a contract, because the
chances of that happening lie somewhere between slim
and none.

- Ask about security. Reports of burglaries would suggest
that it is good to be cautious. In some apartment buildings,
residents deter thieves by installing metal security gates over
the doors to their apartments. If your neighbors are doing
this, you should probably follow suit.

- Clarify whether there are management or parking fees that
must be paid in addition to rental fees. Especially when
renting from a private "landlord" in a villa complex or an
apartment building, pay a visit to the management office to
confirm that there are no extra fees that will spring up on
you later.

In spite of all your best efforts to confirm details, be prepared
for just about anything to happen. Upon arriving in Beijing, an
expat executive and her spouse were told that their apartment
wasn't quite ready yet. They lived in a hotel for over two weeks,
eagerly anticipating the move into their new apartment. As soon
as they were told the apartment was ready, they packed up their
things. The next morning, the executive headed off to work and
her husband loaded their belongings into a taxi and went to the
apartment. Walking into the apartment, he felt the floor squish
beneath his feet. A pipe had burst overnight, and the entire
apartment was flooded. At least the couple's belongings were still
in the taxi and were safe from the flooding.

TELEPHONES

Fixed Telephone Lines
It used to be that having to make two or three telephone calls to other parts of Beijing—even to the next building—could take all day. Imagine the impact that the improved telephone service has had on productivity in Beijing! Some issues remain, however.

The first has to do with demand. Because of competition from mobile (cellular) telephones, among other factors, fixed telephone lines are being promoted heavily. Even installation fees have been abolished. Thus, don't be surprised if you are told that it will take one month to get telephone service turned on after you have made your final housing selection. This is meant to be a generous estimate; depending on demand that month, it is more likely that your telephone line will be installed within 10–20 days.

Another issue has to do with connectivity, although this is not expected to continue much longer. A couple of areas in Beijing have outdated switching systems, and making telephone calls into or out of these areas of the city can be difficult. There is really nothing that can be done about this directly. You cannot just contact the telephone company and ask them to fix the problem; instead, you must find ways to circumvent it. The easiest way is to get a mobile phone. (Incidentally, back when most neighborhoods in the city used the old systems and no one had mobile phones yet, people often gave up on trying to use their telephones and instead just went to see the person they were trying to call. Indeed, perhaps one of the reasons that Chinese people sometimes show up to talk without calling in advance is that they have had years of frustrating experiences with their domestic telephone system.)

While many Chinese people get only DDD (domestic direct dial) lines installed in their homes, expats usually have IDD (international direct dial) lines installed. IDD service includes DDD service. Expats from industrialized nations on corporate assignments generally want at least two IDD lines — one for the telephone and one for the fax and computer. (Most expats have a fax at home. See the chapter on *Working in Beijing* concerning issues of confidentiality and privacy.)

Public Telephones

More public telephones become available every day in Beijing. Many of them are simply private lines made public. For example, a neighborhood vendor of soda and candy will acquire a DDD line for his or her kiosk, put up a sign in Chinese that says "public telephone," and charge a small fee for calls made. Very often, though, these public phones are for local calls only; long distance and international calls must be made from other phones. These can be found at the Beijing Long Distance Call Building, at the airport and at other locations around the city.

There are several different ways to use public telephones. One is to use a telephone card, which is for sale at most newspaper kiosks around the city. Sometimes they are sold at a discount relative to the amounts designated on the cards. Other special cards for long distance calls can also be purchased. Not all phone cards work on all public telephones. Check with other expats after you have arrived in Beijing to learn which types of telephone cards are most convenient at that moment.

Mobile Telephones

Instead of using public telephones, though, most people get mobile (cellular) telephones. In worldwide rankings, China is high on the list in terms of the overall number of users of mobile phones. Everyone who is anyone carries one. Prices for mobile phones and services are on a par with those in other countries. Mobile phones purchased in other countries and Chinese territories cannot be used without a local SIM card.

Telephone Directories

Accurate and useful residential telephone directories in English do not exist in Beijing. There are, however, a few reputable and useful English-language business telephone directories, some of which are published in Hong Kong. One of the best is *The China Phone Book & Business Directory*. In case you ever get stuck while you are out wandering around the city and need a business address or telephone number, keep in mind that many of the major hotels have this directory in their business centers.

Due to the absence of residential telephone directories, most expats exchange business cards. As soon as you have selected your residence and know what your telephone number and address will be, have family business cards made with English on one side and Chinese on the other. These cards can be passed out to friends, associates, and merchants who must make deliveries to your home, and to family members who will want to call you or send you mail while you are living in Beijing.

Internet

Broadband services and high speed lines are now being offered to meet the needs of Internet users in some residential and most office buildings catering to expats and foreign companies. While reasonably priced, such services should be tested before committing to the service to determine if the speed and connectivity can be delivered as promised.

UTILITIES

Methods of payment for utilities such as gas, water, heat, and electricity vary greatly. Most expats pay a yearly lump sum or a monthly fee to the property management organization to cover all utilities. Others pay by metered rates, and utility employees come into their homes to read the meters once per month. A few days later, utility employees come again (usually around dinner time) to collect payment in cash.

Certain types of homes, especially apartments, require the payment of maintenance fees to cover various costs such as having a guard to watch the building, hiring someone to clean public areas such as hallways, hiring someone to cut the grass and/or do landscaping, and providing garbage removal.

If cable television is available, the cost for the basic Chinese-language cable package of about 30 channels is relatively inexpensive. Usually this is paid once per year, and someone will visit your home to collect the payment in cash. The international cable package is not available in every area of Beijing.

※ ※ ※

The housing situation described in this chapter pertains primarily to expats, and particularly to foreigners. People from other parts of China, in most cases, are not free to move to Beijing and establish permanent, independent residences. One reason for this is that no housing has been officially allocated to these individuals. Chinese citizens must obtain a housing permit in order to legitimately relocate to Beijing from other parts of China.

There are plenty of homes from which expats can choose in Beijing these days. It is likely that the process of selecting a residence will only become more complex as time goes by and restrictions on where expats can live are relaxed. No matter what type of housing they choose, many build in the option to move after the first year or so. Some expats find that after they have lived in Beijing for a while, their housing no longer suits their needs. Knowing more about themselves and the city, they can then make arrangements to move to a more suitable environment.

— CHAPTER FIVE—

GETTING SETTLED

Getting settled in a new place is never easy. It can be a challenge
to simultaneously maintain connections with people and things
that you cherish from the past while building the foundation for a
new life. Preparing and packing in an effective way can alleviate
some of the stress. Practical measures, such as arranging care of
personal finances, can also make your new life more manageable.
In Beijing, domestic help is an option that can relieve you of the
more tedious chores of daily life. When hired and managed
appropriately, domestic help can be a tremendous resource to
newcomers in Beijing.

PREPARING AND PACKING

Most people move to another country with just their personal belongings. After all, isn't the process of procuring new furniture and appliances half the fun of an international move? Other people make more encumbered, "corporate" moves. In other words, they take half their belongings with them, including furniture, and put the other half into storage in their home countries for the duration of the assignment. Either way, it is assumed that readers of this book will receive some type of assistance with the moving process. Organizations that provide such assistance, such as relocation companies, usually have their own lists of recommendations about what to take with you and what to leave at home, but here are some additional guidelines.

Music and Videos

For starters, most expats moving to Beijing take their entire music collections with them. The good thing about cassette tapes and CDs is that you can play them on any system. Videos are a different story. Those taken to Beijing from Japan, some countries in Europe, and the United States cannot be played on Chinese systems unless they are multi-system units. (The video system used in China is PAL. Japan and the United States use the NTSC system, and some countries such as France use SECAM.) It is possible to purchase multi-system televisions and VCRs in many major cities of the world such as Tokyo, New York, or Hong Kong, but it is probably best to wait and buy them in Beijing. You might even decide to purchase a DVD or VCD player rather than a VCR after you have arrived, as the selection of movies available in these formats is much greater than that of videos.

Mementos

Take lots of mementos of your home country to hand out as gifts during your time in Beijing. Some suggested items are:

- postage stamps that commemorate something about your home culture
- glossy-paged books of photos of your home city or region
- locally-made crafts or trinkets
- packages of postcards depicting famous sites in your home country or town

Furniture

If you want at least one piece of your own furniture in Beijing, take your bed, especially if you are tall or are used to sleeping on a very large mattress such as that of a king-sized bed. And if you take a Western king-sized bed, you'd better include some sheets as well. Even though China makes king-sized sheets for export, you're not likely to find them available there for sale.

Clothing

The system of sizes used for labeling clothes found in stores geared toward Chinese people is different from the system used for clothing that is meant to be sold in Western countries. Although some of the local markets sell factory overruns in sizes for Westerners, expats who are especially large or tall might want to take most of their own clothing with them to Beijing. Some of the items that are difficult, if not impossible, to find in the city include very long-legged trousers, very large-sized shoes, tall- or queen-sized pantyhose, and anything larger than an A-cup bra. While casual clothing is relatively easy to buy locally, professional business attire is not so easy to find. Some expats get replicas of their favorite business suits made by tailors at the Friendship Stores and other places.

Books and Magazines

People who do not speak English as their native language might want to take novels and other reading materials from their home countries. (Most of the foreign language materials for sale in Beijing are produced in English.) Also useful are reference materials such as a good dictionary in your own language, a bilingual dictionary in your native language and Chinese, a detailed map of your home country, and a world atlas.

People with special interests or hobbies, such as cooking and gardening, should take reference books and other hard-to-find instructional materials from home.

Don't take any politically sensitive books, or anything that could vaguely be construed as pornography. For example, it is best to leave at home your copies of books chronicling first-person experiences during the Cultural Revolution and the Tiananmen incident. Discontinue your subscription to *Playboy*, because it will be confiscated before it can ever arrive at your home in Beijing.

Household Appliances

Also, don't bother taking any appliances such as hair dryers, blenders, microwaves, computers, televisions, or stereo systems unless they are made to use the same voltage that is available in China (220 volts/50 hertz), or unless they can accommodate multiple voltage systems. Appliances that are not manufactured to be compatible with the electrical system used in China must be run on transformers, and even then many appliances will not work properly. As power spikes can happen in Beijing, be sure to use surge protectors to safeguard valuable equipment.

Pets

Only petite pets such as birds, fish, cats, and small dogs are officially permitted in the urban districts of Beijing. (Some pets need to be licensed. Larger animals may be permitted in suburban and rural areas. Check with authorities or other expats for more details after you arrive.) Birds were by far the most popular pets among Chinese people until recent years. Often, older people can be seen around the city taking their birds out for fresh air and exercise, or to meet up with other birds. Many Chinese bird owners believe that their pets sing more beautifully when they have other birds around to encourage them.

A Beijing resident takes his birds for their morning "walk."

More and more people can be seen walking dogs in the evening, and some grocery stores now regularly stock pet food for cats and dogs. However, we really do not recommend taking pets to Beijing—especially furry ones. First of all, any international flight is likely to be too long to be humane for an animal. Secondly, some people have lost their pets while living in Beijing. As there are relatively few pets in the city, one might think that it would be easy to find one that's missing. It is possible that a couple of them became an evening meal. The more you cherish your pet, the more you should reconsider taking it with you to Beijing.

Instead, find a new pet in Beijing. Visit the bird market just north of the Bank of China building in the Fuchengmen neighborhood. There you can find not only birds and bird paraphernalia, but fish and turtles as well, and sometimes other small animals such as tame squirrels, hamsters, and cats. You could also consider adopting a pet from an expat who is headed back home, or helping a furry friend escape from the local produce or meat market. The animals would thank you if they could speak.

Photographs

Last but not least, be sure to take a few photos of friends, family, and familiar places. Not only are they a comfort whenever you're pining for home, but they are also nice to have to show to the new friends you make in China.

PERSONAL FINANCES

Most expats in China do as much of their banking and bill paying as possible in their home countries. One reason is that mail and parcels coming into China are occasionally opened for inspection. It can be uncomfortable to think that Chinese officials might know exactly how much money you have in the bank, that you are behind on your credit card payments, or that you visit a psychic every time you go on home leave. Some expats enlist a trusted friend to help manage their affairs, and others pay a financial advisor to do the job. Technically savvy expats do some of their banking over the Internet. All of these methods offer the benefit of avoiding late payments caused by international postal delays.

If you choose someone to assist with handling your financial affairs, it is a good idea to also give that person legal permission to sign documents for you. (In the United States, for example, this is called granting "power of attorney.") Having a legal signatory at home will avoid tremendous delays in all kinds of matters, as there are some situations in which a faxed signature is unacceptable and only an original will suffice. Even international express mail is not fast enough when you have just two days to submit a financial form with an original signature to your child's preferred university, for example.

Your Salary

Employers in Beijing pay their expats in a variety of ways, depending on the legal structure and nature of their businesses. Salaries may be denominated in foreign currency or in local currency, depending on whether the employer is foreign-owned, Chinese-owned, a joint venture, a representative office, or a wholly-owned entity. Salaries are sometimes paid locally, in which case the employer may offer a method of helping transfer some or all of the funds to an employee's account abroad. Some employers pay abroad, in which case the reverse may be true. Banks in China impose relatively strict controls on the flow of foreign currency, including the disbursement of cash from foreign currency accounts.

When accepting a position in China, be sure to ask in which country and in what currency you will be paid. If you will be paid outside of China, ask your potential employer to assist you in gaining access to funds in Beijing and vice versa. Fees for transferring funds internationally can be quite high, and it generally takes three to five working days for a transfer to be completed and confirmed. Discuss payment methods with your employer so that you are sure to have funds that you can spend in Beijing as well as funds to pay your bills outside the country.

Withdrawing Cash

In Beijing, you can use an ATM card to get cash in local currency, although many ATM machines only work when the branch where they're located is open, and not all ATM machines in Beijing have access to international networks. If you rely on an ATM card for cash, be sure to make arrangements with your financial guardian

81

at home to monitor your bank account balance so that you will always have access to funds when needed.

Yet another way of getting access to cash is to carry an American Express card. If you have a checking account in the United States, you can visit any American Express office during business hours, write a personal check in U.S. dollars and receive local currency at a relatively favorable exchange rate. (For most cardholders, there are weekly limits to the amount that can be obtained.) Check with American Express to see if it offers this service to cardholders from your home country. Cash advances are also possible using credit cards such as Visa and MasterCard, but you might be billed a relatively steep 4–5% surcharge for this service.

Paying Taxes
Be sure to confirm as well how your income will be reported to tax authorities both in China and in your home country. Rules vary widely from country to country, with some requiring citizens working abroad to file a tax return and others requiring nothing at all. But in China, all expats who are residents and are employed for more than three months are required to pay taxes on their income. Employers are required to file and pay China taxes on behalf of their employees. Ask your employer whether the compensation package offered to you is pre-tax or after-tax. Confirm how your employer will report your income, and what sort of documentation you may have to provide (for instance, official tax receipts for rent generally allow one to exclude the cost of renting an apartment from income). Ask to be given copies of all tax documents filed on your behalf. Note that expats who are residents in China for five years or longer may also be subject to taxes on their worldwide income. Those who work as private consultants should heed all rules on paying taxes. The penalties for providing false information to tax authorities are very high.

LOCAL FINANCES

Chinese currency is called *renminbi yuan* — people's currency notes; usually abbreviated as RMB¥ or just RMB. Technically speaking, RMB is a soft currency, which means that it is not traded on international currency exchanges. Depending on the policies of the individual banks in your home country, you may or may not be able to purchase RMB before leaving for Beijing. Likewise, you may or may not be able to sell RMB to banks outside of China. However, some independent money changers will buy and sell RMB. Check with them in advance, as many only carry limited amounts of this currency.

When in China, you will usually be asked to prove that you exchanged hard currency to get RMB, if you want to trade even relatively modest amounts of RMB back to hard currency. A habit that all expats have cultivated is never to throw away receipts that are proof of exchanging hard currency for RMB.

There was a time when foreign exchange certificates (FEC) were used by many expats. Through January 1994, foreigners who exchanged hard currency for Chinese money were given FEC in return. One *yuan* of FEC was equal to one *yuan* of RMB. This system allowed China to micromanage its balance of foreign exchange. With a few exceptions, only FEC could be used to purchase imported goods. In January 1994, China discontinued this dual-currency system and in doing so relaxed (somewhat) its control of the foreign exchange balance. *Renminbi yuan* is the only currency in use in China today.

The term *renminbi* is usually used when contrasting Chinese currency with another type of international currency. The term *yuan* is often used in the written language when referring to units of *renminbi*, and the term *kuai* is used most frequently in the spoken language. Although *yuan* are sometimes referred to as *kuai* by expats, this is not an entirely accurate reference. *Kuai* is actually a "counter." If you have one piece of Chinese money, then you have *yi kuai qian renminbi*, which literally means "one piece of money in people's currency." When people are speaking, though, they often drop the last part of the phrase. Thus, if you ask how much that lovely little wicker basket in the corner of the shop costs, the answer from the shopkeeper might be *yi kuai*, or "one piece." Another way to say *yi kuai qian* (one piece of money) is to say *yi yuan* (one note), but this is more formal and is not commonly used in daily language.

The *yuan* is divided into *jiao* or *mao*, and *fen*.

yuan = RMB1.00

jiao (written term) = *mao* (spoken term) = RMB0.10

fen = RMB0.01

It is a good idea to carry plenty of cash with you at all times when you are in Beijing. All taxicabs, many stores and restaurants, and almost all market vendors in the city only accept cash. You will miss out on some great local restaurants if you insist on paying for everything with plastic.

Many vendors and taxi drivers prefer to be paid with notes in smaller denominations (RMB5 and RMB10), due to occasional troubles with counterfeit currency. Use larger denomination bills (RMB50 and RMB100) at supermarkets, department stores, and hotels, or go to a bank to exchange them for smaller ones.

Credit cards are accepted at most hotels and by services that cater to foreigners. In some cases, when you pay by credit card the merchant will add a surcharge—usually 3-5%—to the price of your purchase in order to cover fees charged by banks and credit card companies. This is likely to occur if you purchase a domestic airline ticket by credit card, for example.

COMMUNICATING WITH HOME

Email

The Internet revolution has almost turned the issue of

communicating with home while on an expat assignment into a non-issue. Email has drastically reduced the anxiety caused by leaving family members behind, particularly for expats who want to stay in touch with an elderly family member. It is now easy and inexpensive to communicate with loved ones on a daily basis. No hassles; less guilt.

However, just because email is convenient, do not let it make you complacent about security. The authorities frown on people using foreign telephone numbers to access the Internet and email, so it is best—not to mention cheaper—to sign up for an account through a local Internet Service Provider (ISP). Local ISPs in Beijing receive transmissions from and send transmissions to official servers. In other words, before your incoming email gets to your ISP and then is delivered to you, it could theoretically be reviewed by the authorities. After email that you are sending out leaves your ISP, it could again, theoretically, be reviewed by authorities before heading toward its final destination. Of course, unless you are conducting an email discussion with friends at home about something incredibly dangerous and threatening such as how to make a pipe bomb, you probably do not need to worry about the authorities scrutinizing your email traffic. Many expats, though, are at least somewhat cautious about making overly negative statements concerning life in China, or about expressing criticism of the government.

Also, please be aware that not only can authorities review your email, but they can also restrict your access to certain websites. These are mostly websites that are deemed offensive (such as pornographic sites) or dangerous. If you suddenly cannot get access to a favorite website, keep checking back for a few weeks. Usually within four to six weeks, access to the site will resume as suddenly as it was discontinued.

Snail Mail and Parcels

Despite the convenience of email, it can't meet all your communication needs during a long-term stay in China. Snail mail (old-fashioned air mail) is still a necessity. Most expats have someone, such as a friend or financial advisor, collect mail in their home countries, dispose of junk mail, and then forward the remainder on a regular basis—say, via express mail every two weeks or via air mail once a week. Customs officials periodically open and inspect these types of packages, so again, be sure that any sensitive materials are withheld from shipment.

Larger parcels are a different story. International airmail regulations require that a customs declaration form be attached to any parcels, and officials usually inspect incoming packages. Any parcels that list videotapes in the contents are particularly likely to be opened for inspection, and the videos are sometimes reviewed by Customs officials to be sure they contain no pornography or politically sensitive material. Some expats report that when friends send movies to them in Beijing, the better the movie the longer it takes for them to receive the package.

A positive aspect of the Beijing postal system is that in many urban areas, mail is delivered up to three times a day. (Of course, if you're anxiously awaiting pictures of your new niece or nephew, that's three times a day that you could be disappointed.) Express mail packages sent through the postal systems of most countries are delivered by the Beijing postal service, as are airmail packages. Shipments from courier services such as DHL and UPS do not provide such frequent delivery.

When sending out letters and cards, you must use officially approved envelopes. These come in various sizes and are available for sale at all post offices, as well as in some stationery and department stores. When purchasing envelopes, check on the back for a rectangular box with writing inside that confirms the envelopes have been approved by the postal service.

Unfortunately, many holiday and birthday cards are sold with unapproved envelopes that cannot be sent through the post, as Chinese people usually deliver these types of cards by hand to relatives, friends, and associates. (In order to mail unapproved envelopes containing cards or letters, you must purchase a larger, official envelope in which to put the original.)

As for sending out mail and parcels, all we can say is that dealing with the Chinese postal system can be a unique experience. The good news is that if you are posting domestic mail, the system is speedy and almost everything arrives. The bad news is that Chinese postal regulations can be variable in terms of what kind of packaging materials must be used, how to address an envelope or parcel, where to write a return address, and where to place a stamp. The first time you attempt mailing any letter or parcel, take advantage of the "human resources" of whatever company, university, or work unit that brought you to Beijing and ask someone there to guide you through the process.

Here is an actual story that illustrates the unique experience of dealing with the postal system in Beijing. It is a translated discussion between an expat (who speaks some Mandarin) and a postal worker, and concerns mailing a parcel from Beijing to Tianjin:

Expat:	*I want to mail this, but I don't have any tape to seal the package. Do you have some?*
Worker:	*Don't have it.* (motions to another window) *She has it.*
Expat:	*Well, could we just weigh it and put the postage on it first? Then I'll go get the tape.*
Worker:	*No. It must be taped first.*
Expat:	(goes to get the tape and returns) *OK. It's ready.*
Worker:	*The address is not in the right place.*
Expat:	*Which address?*

Worker: *Your address. It must be written along the bottom of the package.*

Expat: *But before we always wrote it along the top. And anyway, I don't have any more paper to wrap the package in.*

Worker: *It's a new rule. Just cross it out and write it along the bottom.*

This situation was confusing and frustrating even for an expat who spoke Mandarin! So first of all, don't blame all of your communication troubles during your first few months in Beijing on the fact that you don't speak Mandarin or that you don't perfectly understand Beijing dialect. Secondly, don't expect that you will figure out everything about Beijing just by reading this book or that you'll know what to do based on your accumulated life experiences. Even after you've gotten used to many things in your new home, changes will occur. Try to be as flexible as possible—especially at the post office.

RESOLVING HOUSING ISSUES

When things go wrong in your new home, it can sometimes be difficult to determine how to get help. Prepare yourself to handle such problems by asking the rental agent for clarification before you sign a rental agreement. In most cases, if you live in housing designated for foreigners, problems are handled by contacting the management company of the building or complex.

The quality of service and timeliness of response can vary widely and are usually better the more one is paying for housing. It is a good idea to be at home when repair staff or technicians visit your residence and to supervise their work closely, although many expats have the *ayi* supervise these visits instead. You could be charged for repairs, so clarify what types of repairs are covered by the "landlord" when you sign your rental agreement.

Occasionally, of course, nothing can be done when certain problems occur. If work is being conducted on the gas lines or electrical system in your neighborhood, you probably won't know about it in advance, but your Chinese neighbors might—the authorities put announcements of this type of work in the Chinese-language newspapers. For example, one of these announcements might advise that the electrical supply to your neighborhood will be interrupted from 9 a.m. to noon on Wednesday. Thus, your first recourse should always be to ascertain whether other people in your apartment building, housing complex, or neighborhood are experiencing the same problem that you are.

As for discussing housing problems, when you are among other expats, it is acceptable—indeed it is common—to complain. This includes the quality issues mentioned earlier, as well as infrastructure failure (electricity blackouts, for example) and housing malfunctions (such as doors that do not open or close properly, or drains that do not work well). However, complaining about these issues to or in the presence of local colleagues and friends is not recommended. Compared with the housing in which many local people live, you are probably living in a palace.

DOMESTIC HELPERS

Many expats living in Beijing hire at least one *ayi*, which is a "domestic helper" or a woman who helps with household chores. (More literally, this word means "auntie." Some people use the term *amah*, which is derived from Portuguese and is used in other parts of Asia to mean "domestic helper.") An individual *ayi* is some-times hired to fill only one of three functions—housekeeping (general cleaning as well as laundry), childcare, or food shopping and preparation; other *ayis* fill more than one role. Some *ayis* are employed full-time, working nine hours or so per day, five days a week; others work for several expat families and visit each home only once or twice per week. Occasionally an *ayi* will live in the expat home, but most often she lives in her own home with her family.

It is best not to rush the process of hiring an *ayi*. Unlike in other countries where domestic helpers are found through agencies, in Beijing they are most often found via word of mouth. Take your time getting recommendations from other expats. This way, you might be able to find an *ayi* who is already accustomed to the habits of people from your home country. Ask expats who refer *ayis* to you about their general experiences with the *ayis*, as well as asking about more specific issues such as what appliances the *ayis* are accustomed to using.

Once you have received a good recommendation, arrange an interview with the *ayi*. For people who do not speak Mandarin, it is a good idea to have an interpreter present to assist with the interview. Here are some questions you might want to ask:

- What part of China is she from? If you are planning to hire her for childcare and she does not speak standard Mandarin, her accent and vocabulary use might influence the development of your children's abilities in the Chinese language.
- How long has she lived in Beijing? When problems arise, an *ayi* who has lived in Beijing for a long time is more likely to have a variety of resources at her disposal to resolve them than is a newcomer.
- How much experience does she have in working with expats? Some experience is good, but too much experience with a single family might mean that she thinks she knows what all expats want and might be resistant to trying new things.
- Does she have a child? If so, then she probably has more experience caring for children than does a younger *ayi* who does not yet have a child of her own.

- What does she enjoy about working with expats?
- What does she find challenging about working with expats?
- If the *ayi* will be helping with children, it is a good idea to ask about her health. Pay particular attention to any signs of jaundice (this might indicate hepatitis) or excessive coughing (which could indicate tuberculosis).
- How will she get to your home each day? Some expats must arrange for their drivers to pick up their *ayis* either before or after taking working spouses to the office.
- How can she be contacted during off hours? In an emergency (for example if one of your children gets sick), you might need the *ayi* to stay with the other child while you take the sick one to the doctor. If the *ayi* gives you a telephone number where you can reach her, make a test call to her the following day. During the interview process, some expats even go to see the place where the *ayi* lives in case they should ever need to fetch her at odd hours.

If you plan to have the *ayi* cook for you and your family, be sure to test her abilities by asking her to cook a sample meal before you make your final decision. Dietary restrictions and other food considerations should be mentioned during the interview process.

In terms of compensation, again it is a good idea to discuss this issue with a few expat families to learn what they are paying for their *ayis*. Chinese people talk openly with each other about compensation. If word spreads that you are paying too much, other expat families are likely to pressure you to lower the amount because their *ayis* will be demanding more money. If you pay too little, you could be the subject of gossip because it could be perceived that you are exploiting your domestic employees.

Define the responsibilities of the *ayi* carefully, and expect to spend a few months resolving misunderstandings in this area. Expats from countries in which individual initiative is expected might find that the *ayi* follows instructions too literally, and does not adjust her habits as circumstances change. Other expats from more hierarchical cultures might be surprised when the *ayi* openly disagrees with recommendations and instructions. In any case, do not leave the *ayi* unsupervised for at least the first few weeks of her employment. Time invested in preparing and training the *ayi* to work in the unique environment of your home will pay off in the long run.

The relatively low cost of domestic help makes it common for expats living in Beijing to hire one or more *ayis*. Managing domestic help, however, can be stressful if expectations are not clearly outlined and periodically reinforced. Also, when there is more than one *ayi* in the home, infighting and power plays can occur and require mediation by the employer. Some expats who start out with more than one *ayi* eventually retain only a single, efficient *ayi* to reduce the time and stress involved in *ayi* management. Other expats are quite successful at training multiple *ayis* to manage their homes and chores with minimal supervision.

Expats who take appliances and other items from their home countries to Beijing should enlist the assistance of a bilingual person to label in Chinese the indicators and settings on those appliances, and perhaps to write out in Chinese any complicated instructions for their use. It is also a good idea to label in Chinese any cleaning products, chemicals, or medicines that you have around the house.

Those who hire an *ayi* for childcare should take some special precautions. Provide detailed instructions to the *ayi* for cases of emergency. Take the *ayi* to visit your pediatrician at least once so that the doctor is not a stranger to her. Take her to the hospital to which you would prefer your children be taken in a medical emergency. Be sure that your *ayi* is introduced to neighbors who can assist in a crisis. Put emergency phone numbers, labeled in Chinese, next to the telephone.

A complaint frequently mentioned by expats who hire an *ayi* for childcare is that the *ayi* lets the children do anything they want. Many *ayis* hesitate to discipline the children of their employers unless they have been explicitly instructed to do so. There is a tendency toward a laissez-faire approach to child rearing in Chinese culture and most children are indulged when they are very young. In China, however, the one-child policy has created what some call "little emperors and empresses." Children tend to be spoiled—not just by their parents, but by two sets of grandparents and other adults as well. Be explicit with the *ayi* about things that your children are allowed and not allowed to do. Be specific about how much and what kinds of food they can eat. One result of Chinese kids being spoiled is that obesity has become a relatively widespread problem in China.

Despite some of the challenges of *ayi* management, many expats come to rely on them for advice, information, and insights into the Chinese environment. The eventual parting of an expat family and an *ayi* can be tearful and fraught with emotion, but an assortment of wonderful memories can be the reward for your mutual association.

DRIVERS

Many expats—especially those sent to Beijing by multinational companies—are not allowed to drive during their stays, so they hire drivers. Some drivers speak a bit of English, and very occasionally it is possible to find drivers who speak other foreign languages. Most of the drivers in Beijing, however, speak only Mandarin, and almost all of them are male.

The local branches of the organizations that send expats to China usually assist in hiring drivers. Working expats who replace people who have returned to their home countries will probably not have much of a choice in the hiring process, as they will be assigned the drivers of their predecessors. If you do need to hire a

93

driver, be sure to ask some of the following questions during interviews. The rationales for these questions are similar to those when hiring an *ayi*.

- What part of China is he from?
- How long has he lived in Beijing?
- How much experience does he have in working with expats?
- Does he have a child? If he will be taking your children around the city, he will have a better idea how to interact with them appropriately if he has a child of his own.
- What does he enjoy about working with expats?
- What does he find challenging about working with expats?
- How is his health?
- Did previous employers take any weekend trips? This question will give you an indication of the driver's flexibility in terms of being available to you on weekends, and will also tell you if he is familiar with getting to locations outside Beijing.

Although *ayis* have predetermined schedules most days of the week, drivers are more often asked to go with the unpredictable flow of a busy professional's workday. The mealtimes of drivers are often interrupted or delayed by the need to ferry employers to lunch or dinner meetings. Last minute changes in schedule are common. These situations can lead to friction with even the most flexible of drivers. Setting up guidelines in advance for handling overtime as well as miscellaneous costs, such as the driver's meal when away from the office, can help avoid misunderstandings later. Senior executives who pack their schedules from early morning to late at night are sometimes assigned two drivers to handle the extra demands.

It is a good idea to maintain some personal distance from both drivers and *ayis*. Expats from relatively egalitarian cultures should be cautious about welcoming them to be members of their households. In one instance, a driver was invited by an expat family to come in and make himself at home whenever he was waiting for his next assignment. One afternoon, the non-working spouse came back from a neighbor's home and found the driver stretched out on the couch with a beer in his hand.

PERSONAL SERVICES

Traditionally, relatively few services such as catering and delivery have been available in Beijing, although they are proliferating now. As with so many other things, the best way to learn about them is by word of mouth and personal recommendations. Other methods include subscribing to an online newsletter or picking up one of the English-language magazines for expats (such as *City Weekend*).

A father waits while his son gets a haircut.

95

These can usually be found in the lobbies of hotels, restaurants, and office buildings frequented by expats.

As for beauty services, several hotels host salons that use imported products — many local salons do not carry products, such as hair coloring, that are suitable for non-Asians. People with naturally curly hair would be well advised to frequent the hotel salons, as only Chinese beauticians who have special training can cut curly hair. Many expat men also use the services offered by hotel-based salons, although a few use the local option of getting their hair cut by a street barber.

✱✱✱

When moving to a new country, many people have the naïve notion that they will be completely settled within a month or so. With all that is involved in getting situated in your new home in Beijing, do not be surprised if you do not feel organized and comfortable for the entire first year. Once you have everything in place, though, it will have been well worth the wait. In the meantime, explore the city. The sooner you do, the sooner it will feel like home.

Chapter Six

GETTING AROUND BEIJING

TRIGG

Navigating Beijing might require more adjustment than you expect. But the city offers plenty of options: walking, driving, taking taxis, bicycling, or riding the trains and subway. No matter which mode you choose, getting out allows you to feel the pulse of the city and see how Beijingers live.

"RULES" FOR PEDESTRIANS

During their first visits to Beijing, many expats are terrified to cross the streets. It seems like traffic comes at them in a completely haphazard fashion. A little fear is probably a healthy thing, as it makes one cautious—but in Beijing traffic, assertiveness is the only way to get where you want to go. Of course, being assertive does not mean being reckless. There are some unwritten "rules" that folks in Beijing follow both to get ahead and to avoid being run over by cars, bicycles, and buses.

An unwritten rule for pedestrians is to use crossing lights as guidelines only. Just because the light is flashing in your favor does not mean that it's safe to cross the street. Always look before stepping into the crosswalk to avoid getting tangled up in the stream of bicycles. (In Beijing, the outer lanes on each side of the major streets are theoretically for bicycles only.) When you see a break in the flow of bicycles, take a big step forward. Hopefully you will notice that the flow of bicycles has curved so that it passes behind you, and you can continue to the edge of the street that you want to cross.

One of the most dangerous things you can do is to get to the edge of the car lanes, watch the crossing light, and step out as soon as it changes. Frankly, this is likely to get you killed. In Beijing, as in many other Chinese cities, cars can turn right on a red light—but unlike in most foreign cities, cars in China are not obligated to stop before turning. Therefore, after the crossing light illuminates, be sure to look for cars turning right before you step into the vehicle lanes, and look for cars turning right onto the street you are crossing as you approach the opposite side.

Until you get used to crossing Beijing streets, the easiest method is to use a local person as your "guide," both literally and figuratively. Find a local person who is preparing to cross the street and position yourself slightly behind the person. Watch the person closely and follow his or her movements exactly as you cross.

Getting through traffic, both for people and vehicles of any kind, is a good metaphor for getting through life in China. There are two other important, unwritten rules. The first is, "If you see an opening, take it. If you don't, someone else will take advantage of your relaxed nature." Thus, some people cross large streets lane by lane with cars zooming around them at full speed. They're just watching for openings in each lane and taking them as they come.

The second is, "Worry only about what is in front of you." It is possible to view this rule being implemented by taxi drivers when they change lanes. The taxi drivers move their cars toward the lanes they want to enter and steadily push the noses of their taxis into the first openings that present themselves. It is the responsibility of any car in those lanes to notice the intervening vehicles and make appropriate accommodations.

"RULES" FOR DRIVERS

Although many diplomats and some employees of small or privately owned companies drive themselves around Beijing, other foreign residents do not. When they need to travel by car, they either take taxis or hire dedicated drivers with cars. Some expats drive themselves to work and on weekend excursions, but prefer to hire a driver to get around the city during the day—using a mobile telephone and laptop computer while riding along, they can make the most of critical work hours. Foreign students, of course, generally cannot afford to purchase cars and drive in Beijing.

Certain expats are forbidden to drive by their employers because there is uncertainty about the penalties that might be imposed on foreigners when traffic accidents occur. As most multinational companies with offices or operations in Beijing send expats to China for only one or two years, corporate executives are concerned about long-term responsibility for damages, injuries, and casualties imposed as a result of traffic accidents. (The responsibility might not end with the departure of the employees from China. Instead, the employers might be required to bear the long-term fulfillment of this responsibility.) In traditional Chinese thinking, these potential responsibilities are:

- A driver who injures another person could be liable for paying the injured person's medical expenses.
- A driver who disables another person could be liable for supporting the disabled person for the rest of that person's life, no matter what the person's age when the accident occurred.
- A driver who kills a working adult who has dependents could be liable for financially supporting all of those dependents (parents, spouse, and/or children) for the rest of their lives.

In China, laws tend to be vaguely written, and previously imposed penalties are not always used as binding precedents or even as guidelines in future legal decisions. Without clear laws and predictable penalties, most multinationals simply forbid their employees to drive while living in Beijing, as well as in most other cities of China.

Often, expats who are used to driving in their home countries and who cannot drive while in Beijing sense a loss of independence and control. Some go through periods during which they avoid going anywhere by car because they are so tired of having to either make arrangements with the family driver or deal with recalcitrant taxi drivers. Some expats miss driving so much that they fantasize about getting into a car, turning up the radio, and driving with the wind whipping through their hair.

If you decide to drive, watch out at all times for bicyclists near your vehicle. They can appear quickly, and hitting one can be quite a messy and sorry affair. Be careful to obey traffic rules, as most intersections now have cameras to record infractions. (Often, drivers are not told that they have infractions on their records until they attempt to renew their driver's license. More than three infractions can prevent drivers from getting their license renewed.) Pay attention to traffic lights, but if a police officer enters the intersection you should give that police officer your attention as well—a police officer directing traffic will have priority over the lights.

When a driver is pulled over by a police officer, the driver is expected to get out of the vehicle and approach the officer. The officer will then advise the driver of the infraction, perhaps questioning the driver or imposing a fine. Expat folklore has long held that it is best not to speak Mandarin with police officers if you want to avoid a ticket or fine, but it is uncertain whether this tactic actually works. In any case, politeness and deference are far more likely to spare the driver than are defensiveness, arguments, or anger.

Driving while intoxicated is taken seriously in Beijing, and from time to time checkpoints are established to catch drunk drivers. The availability and low cost of taking taxis make drinking and driving easy to avoid. Last but not least, please note that drivers are forbidden to smoke or use mobile phones while driving.

It is possible nowadays to rent cars but only if you have a residency permit and a Chinese driver's license. In general, to get a Chinese driver's license, one must complete an application, pass a health test, produce the residency permit, and surrender a foreign driver's license. Check with the foreigners' section of the automotive division of the Public Transportation Management Bureau on obtaining a Chinese driver's license.

By the way, traffic in Beijing flows on the right, as it does in countries such as Germany, Canada, and the United States.

TAXIS

Dealing with taxi drivers has long been a frustrating fact of life for expats and Beijingers alike. The situation is getting better, especially during tourist season when drivers are busy and making money. But if you have had even one encounter with them when business is slow, you probably have a good idea of what we mean.

101

Beijing traffic moving along the Second Ring Road.

Some taxi drivers act as though their riders owe them more than the metered fare for a trip from one point to another. Although tipping is officially against the rules in China, Beijing taxi drivers have been known to try to "innocently" get a little extra fare from a rich expat, which in this case means anyone who is from a "wealthy" industrialized country. Here are some antidotes to their ploys.

Let's say that a taxi driver just brought you from the Beijing University campus to the Kempinski Hotel, and the fare was RMB74. You have only an RMB100 note in your wallet, so you give this to the driver. The oldest trick in the Beijing cabbie's book is, "Oops. Sorry. No change." This happens so frequently that, with time, it can make even the most patient resident fly into a rage; but it is also the easiest taxi problem to remedy. As mentioned earlier, always carry small denomination (RMB10, RMB5, RMB2, and RMB1) notes with you so that you can offer exact change.

However tempting it might be, don't spend these smaller bills for purchases at department stores or the like. In this case, hopefully you can give the driver the exact fare of RMB74. If that's not possible, then give the driver RMB75 or RMB80—but don't expect to get any change back.

The Beijing airport is famous for taxi shenanigans. Coming out of the baggage claim area, foreigners are targets for hustlers. The best defense is to simply ignore their chants of "Taxi? Taxi?" Many of them are not even official taxi drivers; some are drivers who "borrow" cars when they're not needed by their *danwei* (work units) and then split any proceeds of their entrepreneurial efforts with the work unit. As these cars have no meters, only if you speak Mandarin fluently and know the exact fare to your destination should you dare to negotiate with these hustlers.

Exiting the airport building, head for the official taxi line. When you're seated in the car, look for the meter. Often the driver will have covered it with an innocent-looking lace doily, hoping that the passenger will not notice it and insist that it be turned on. Inquire about the meter and request that it be used. (Riders who do not speak Mandarin can just point to the dashboard area and say "Meter?" in English.) If you do not take these steps of searching for the meter and indicating that you want it to be started up, you are at risk of being charged at least double for your ride. If the driver says the meter is broken, simply get out of the car and find another taxi. The meter sometimes magically repairs itself when this happens!

Guilt trips sometimes accompany taxi trips, especially for foreigners. If you speak a bit of Mandarin, the taxi driver might ask you seemingly innocent questions such as where you are from and how much airfare from your home country to China costs. "Oh," might be the driver's reply, "did you know that your airfare to China costs more than a person like me makes in a year?" Additional questions and conversation about relative wealth will ensue, and upon arriving at your destination the taxi driver will plead for a little extra fare because, "You can afford it."

Other taxi driver scams include taking unsuspecting passengers on circuitous routes to their destinations; accepting advance payment to wait for passengers and then leaving; demanding an additional fee halfway to the destination and dropping off, in the middle of nowhere, the passenger who refuses to pay this extra fee; the list goes on and on. Probably the most extreme practice is rigging the meter so that it records more miles or time than actually is the case — and this ruse, experienced Beijing residents concur, is the hardest to do anything about. The bottom line is, when you get into a Beijing taxi, be savvy and aware; don't let down your guard just because someone else is doing the driving.

Granted, some things that happen to foreigners in Beijing taxis aren't the fault of local drivers. Many of the taxis displaying the cheapest fares (the rate per kilometer is posted on the side windows of the car) are driven by people who are not from Beijing. Often they are new to the city and don't know the roads and landmarks well. It is best to avoid these cars unless you know the best route to your destination and can speak enough Mandarin to guide the driver.

Incidentally, it can be difficult even for experienced local taxi drivers to find Beijing locations on the basis of a name and street address alone — among other reasons, place names in English do not necessarily match or even resemble the names in Chinese, and street numbers are often not sequential. Drivers will complain loud and long if you ask them to find a location on the basis of just a name and address, as they do not want to be blamed if the location cannot be found.

Most long-term residents of Beijing know that the best way to find a location they have not visited before is to have someone who knows the location take them there first. As an example, let's say that you attend a party and mention that you are interested in wool carpets. If another expat says that she knows a great place that the tourists haven't yet discovered, instead of asking where the place is or copying the name and address from the place's business card that she shows you, ask her to let you know the next time she goes there and to take you along.

In addition to having someone accompany you on your first visit to a new location, another good way to get to a new location is to provide the driver with a map identifying in Chinese characters the location you wish to find, street intersections, and nearby landmarks. Foreigners who live in buildings that are not well-known often have business cards printed that include their address in Chinese on one side and a small map on the other. Occasionally the landmarks and directions given by expats living in Beijing are rather amusing–"turn left at the purple public toilets."

When it is not possible to provide your driver with a map, ask someone who speaks Mandarin for help in describing the location to the taxi driver. If this person can tell the taxi driver that the location is a store where foreigners like to buy carpets from Xinjiang, for example, the driver might then recognize it. If not, the driver might just try to guess the neighborhood of the location and take you there. Then the driver will use the clue about foreigners buying Xinjiang carpets to ask people in the neighborhood for help finding the location.

Another method for visiting new locations is to ask to be taken to the best known landmark near the place you're looking for and set off on foot from there. Long-term residents who speak Mandarin employ this tactic even for places that they can describe in Chinese, because it is so difficult to accurately designate locations for drivers. An additional factor that complicates the whole matter is that there are many stretches along large avenues where taxi drivers are forbidden to drop passengers. You will just have to get out of the taxi and walk that half block to your favorite hole-in-the-wall Shandong restaurant.

When going on excursions outside the city, be cautious about negotiating privately to hire a taxi for the day. Fares that are negotiated privately usually seem like better deals than they really are. With new highways and toll booths being added practically every day, neither taxi drivers nor expats can keep up with all the changes. It is thus nearly impossible to negotiate fares that include tolls—and depending on your destination, these could wipe out the fortune you think you're saving. Smaller taxis certainly seem like they'll save you even more money, but they also lack effective shock absorbers and probably air-conditioning or heating as well. Carefully consider whether you can tolerate an extended ride in such discomfort. To make matters worse, many of these smaller cars sputter when climbing the slightest of inclines and cannot reach highway speed limits. Some drivers lean forward trying to speed up their vehicles with a little body English, but it's doubtful this has much impact.

A day trip usually necessitates having at least one meal away from Beijing. As most taxi drivers do not personally know of good restaurants outside the city, they will often take you to places that have a reputation for serving meals to foreign tourists. Unfortunately, these restaurants also have a reputation for conning expats and tourists with such tricks as handing them a menu with a prix fixe lunch starting at RMB150 per person—about 50% more than the total price of a typical meal for two at a moderately priced local restaurant in Beijing. Another trick is to push a certain dish as the "specialty of the house" or "special of the day," and then charge an exorbitant price for it. In the end, the easiest way to take a day trip outside Beijing is to make arrangements with a legitimate organization, such as a hotel or tourist office, for a package deal. It will probably cost at least twice as much as the car fare that you could negotiate privately, plus a slightly-higher-than-normal price for lunch, but you'll have a speedy ride in comfort and will know the total cost in advance.

If any taxi driver really gives you trouble, you can write down the license number from the identification card posted on the front dashboard and announce that you will report the driver to the authorities. Some people do this only as a warning. Such a report is quite a serious thing, as a total of three complaints will strip the driver of her or his taxi license. In any case, the fine print of the taxi rules states that if the driver does not go by the meter, the passenger has the option not to pay the fare.

Always get and keep receipts when taking taxis in case you leave something in the car, or in case you change your mind and decide later to make a complaint about the driver. The receipt will show the name of the operating company of the car, and possibly the license plate number. But even when you argue with a taxi driver or are dissatisfied with the service, try to remain calm and end on a neutral note. People most often forget and leave their belongings in taxis when they have been caught up in some sort of dispute with the driver.

On the positive side, Beijing taxi drivers are pretty safe conversational partners for expats who speak limited Mandarin and want to try out their language skills. For foreigners who speak Mandarin more fluently, they are a constant source of free-style updates on whatever is happening among the common people of Beijing. In preparation for the 2008 Olympics, some taxi drivers are studying foreign languages with renewed interest.

BICYCLES AND WALKING

There are many things that you can experience only by spending time biking and walking around Beijing. Among these are the sights and smells of the *hutong*, which are the essence of the old city. A cluster of grannies gossips about the neighbors. People go about their daily lives in *siheyuan* (courtyard homes). A postal worker yells for people to come and get their mail. Itinerant vendors peddle their wares.

107

Biking around Beijing is a wonderful experience and can give expats a feeling of independence. If your bicycle breaks down, you can get it fixed at one of the makeshift repair shops that appear on practically every corner. Please be forewarned that a long ride on a Chinese-made bicycle can result in your having to sit on pillows for a few days afterward. The seats are very hard, and the sidewalks and roads can be bumpy. Thus, some expats buy padded bicycle seats in their home countries for use in Beijing.

Two grannies chat next to pedicabs out for a tour of the hutong.

For bicyclists, dismounting when passing through the entry gates to buildings or complexes used to be mandatory. It is no longer mandatory in most cases, but it is now considered polite behavior to dismount and walk your bicycle through entryways.

Biking can have its treacherous side. Be careful to observe all of the *"Rules" for Pedestrians* mentioned earlier in this chapter: use traffic signals and crossing lights as guidelines only; watch out for cars turning right when the traffic signal is red; and pay close attention to what is in front of you. Be patient with other bicyclists—the sheer volume of them means that minor accidents happen with some frequency. One survey estimated the number of bicycles in Beijing at approximately 8 million.

Use your bicycle bell when you need to warn other cyclists, as well as pedestrians, of your presence. Despite the risks involved in riding bicycles around Beijing, almost no riders wear safety helmets, including expats. Perhaps this is because traffic tends to move slowly, and serious accidents are not common. It is perfectly acceptable to wear a helmet, though, if you prefer to do so. Reasonably priced helmets are available at some bicycle shops.

Walking can be pleasurable but also difficult, as Beijing is so spread out. Beware that what looks like a five-minute walk on a map may actually take 30 minutes. Both biking and walking, though, are wonderful ways to see the marvels of Beijing.

THE SUBWAY

You should in no way be intimidated by the prospect of riding the *ditie* (subway), also occasionally called the Beijing Metro. It is truly one of the best ways to get around the city. Even if it doesn't go precisely where you want to go, take the subway across town to avoid slow-moving traffic and then take a taxi a short distance to your destination. In fact, the only drawback to taking the subway is that if you pass through the center of the city, you will miss the awesome sight of Tiananmen Square.

The layout of the subway system is simple. The old line or "loop line" follows the Second Ring Road around the city, and several of the stops are named after the old city gates. A second line or "Line 1," completed much later, follows Chang An Avenue (which, as mentioned in the *Welcome to Beijing* chapter, has several names as it traverses the city). The lines cross at the Jianguomen interchange on the east side and at the Fuxingmen interchange on the west side.

In addition to the subway stops shown on the map on page 8, there are eight stops to the west, with Pingguoyuan as the final destination. There are three additional stops to the east, ending with Si Hui East.

The system is relatively easy to navigate. Find a subway entrance, go downstairs, and pay your fare of a few *yuan* at the ticket window. In return, you will receive a paper subway ticket. Hand the ticket to one of the ticket-takers at the top of the stairs leading to the trains. Sometimes they rip the tickets in half and return the stubs, and other times they keep both pieces. Head down the stairs to board the train.

Use the maps posted on the walls to pinpoint the next stop in the direction you want to travel. This will determine from which side of the platform you should board the subway. (The English-language signs indicating the next stop are often hanging over the staircase leading to the platform. If you miss them, and if you do not speak Mandarin, you might have to ask for assistance from other passengers by pointing to the stop you want on a map. Also, please note that on certain signs for Line 1, the direction of the train is indicated by the name of the final stop.) Once you are on the subway train, just before each stop, the name of the next stop will be announced in both Mandarin and English. If you need to change from one line to the other, you will walk through an underground passageway and will not need to buy a new ticket.

When you are ready to come above ground, exits are clearly marked in English. In order to emerge from the subway tunnels at the exit closest to your final destination, look on the subway platform pillars for lists of landmarks accessible from each exit.

TRAINS

Taking a train trip is an excellent way to get out of Beijing for a few days. Most trains depart from two main stations—Beijing Station in the southeast part of town, and Beijing West Station in the southwest. (There are several other train stations in the city as well. Be sure to confirm from which station any train you plan to take will depart. Your final destination determines which station to use.) Four classes of tickets are available and are listed here from cheapest to most expensive: hard seat, hard sleeper, soft seat, and soft sleeper. Seats and sleepers classified as "hard" are plain, hard, unadorned wooden surfaces. Although the soft seats and soft sleepers are the more expensive ways to travel, they are cushioned and are therefore much more comfortable than their "hard" counterparts.

A short ride of a few hours or an overnight trip will take you to fabulous locations such as Qingdao (a seaside city in Shandong Province), Chengde (a summer resort in Hebei Province), or even Xi'an (a former capital of China in Shaanxi Province).

BUSES

The public bus service in Beijing is changing and improving rapidly. Depending on which type of bus you take, it can be an inexpensive way to move around the city. Basically, Beijing has three types of buses.

One type is air-conditioned or heated depending on the weather, and riders are guaranteed seats. This is the most expensive type, but the prices are still a bargain compared with taxis. The second type is neither air-conditioned nor heated, but is usually

111

not overcrowded. The third type is the most economical, but tends to be exceptionally crowded, and riders are hot in the summer and freezing in the winter. Monthly bus passes can be purchased only for the third type of bus. On some buses, an additional fare must be paid when transferring to other buses.

OTHER TRANSPORT OPTIONS

Minibuses are available at most bus stops in Beijing, and the personnel can be aggressive about promoting their services, but it is recommended that outsiders not accept a ride from them. Fares can be inconsistent, and the drivers are not necessarily skilled or experienced. Some people say that these buses are dangerous and full of pickpockets.

Beijing West Railway Station looks spectacular lit up at night.

Pedicabs are yet another Beijing transportation option, but most expats would never want to be seen riding in them. The pedicabs can be found here and there around the city, and are mostly used by tourists trying to travel a few blocks loaded down with the goodies they have bought in the local markets. Fares can be fluid — even with good skills in Mandarin and having negotiated the price in advance, many riders find themselves in a whole new negotiation at the end of the trip. One way of avoiding this is to write down the name of the starting point, the destination, and the price before embarking. Be sure to specify whether the price is per person or for the entire group riding in the pedicab.

* * *

As Beijing is such a sprawling city and it is so common for expats to feel isolated, you should try to become familiar with all transportation options as early as possible in your stay. To assist you in navigating the city, buy a good map in both English and Chinese (the free ones handed out at hotels do not always list enough landmarks and sites to be useful). With the map, you can point out to drivers and other people who do not speak your language the places you want to go. Bon voyage!

Chapter Seven

PERSONAL ISSUES

In particular, working expats in Beijing are generally a privileged lot. They are released from a portion of their domestic responsibilities because most hire *ayis* to at least clean their homes. As many expats do not drive, they are freed from car maintenance responsibilities, not to mention the daily aggravation of navigating Beijing traffic. Although they work long, hard hours during the week, most only toil throughout an entire weekend when they have foreign visitors or Chinese customers in town to entertain. When they have free time, they are at liberty to take advantage of all the amenities that Beijing has to offer.

Yet living in Beijing can require some adjustment, at least for the first year or so. Long hours can keep working expats away from their families, leaving spouses and children to feel abandoned. Learning to manage household staff and other local employees requires time and effort. Working expats who were sent to Beijing because of their successes in commercial endeavors at home, sometimes find that what made them successful before actually leads to failure in China. These situations and others can lead to culture shock and stress.

CULTURE SHOCK

Some of you have probably already experienced a minor version of culture shock. It can happen whenever there is a big change in your life, and especially when that change involves a move to a new location and exposure to new things. For example, when going to a new school or starting a new job, you might have experienced some culture shock.

Much has been written, both academically and anecdotally, about this phenomenon. Basically speaking, culture shock is one's reaction to the ups and downs of adaptation to life in a new culture. It is the process of adjusting to the idea that there is more than one way to look at the world; more than one way to interpret the behavior of another person; more than one way to understand even a single word.

The following is an example of an expat experiencing the first wave of culture shock:

Maria accepted an invitation to be a visiting professor at Qinghua (Tsinghua) University in Beijing for two years. She felt almost euphoric during her first few weeks in the city. It was fall, and the weather was beautiful. Maria did not feel lonely, as she had quickly made friends with other visiting professors at the university. Her Chinese students seemed eager and, unlike her students in Canada, completed all of their assigned projects.

115

About six weeks into her stay, Maria and another visiting professor decided to go to the neighboring city of Tianjin for the weekend. First, however, Maria arranged to have breakfast with a friend of her father's who was in town on business. They met at a hotel, and during breakfast, the staff asked Maria if they could move her travel bag out of the way of other restaurant patrons and put it in an office at the end of the reception counter. Maria agreed. After breakfast, she wanted to do a little shopping, as her train to Tianjin would not leave until 1 p.m. She asked the waitress if she could come back for her bag in a couple of hours. The waitress nodded her head and said, "Mmm."

While Maria was browsing in a department store, she suddenly realized that it was already noon. She raced to the hotel, went to the office where her bag was stored, and discovered that the door was locked. Maria panicked. She was angry, recalling that the waitress had told her it would be all right to come back in a couple of hours.

She rushed up to two employees who were standing behind the reception desk and said, "My bag is in there," pointing to the office. "I need it immediately." The employees looked at each other. One walked away; the other resumed what he had been doing. Maria was furious! How dare they ignore her! "Excuse me," she said, feeling agitated and tapping on the counter, "I need my bag. It's in that office." The employee looked up, said "Wait a moment," and went back to his work. Confused by the lack of a clear response and fearful that she would miss her train, Maria succumbed to frustration; a tear rolled down her cheek.

A few seconds later, the other employee came around the corner with a manager, who unlocked the office and handed Maria her bag. She felt foolish and tried to hide her tears. Managing to utter some words of thanks, she went outside to catch a taxi to the train station. From euphoria to frustration to loss of composure in a matter of minutes—this is evidence of culture shock.

What characterizes the euphoria or "ups" are feelings of success or accomplishment. Before her arrival in Beijing, because she could not speak Mandarin, Maria had been worried about being able to explain assignments clearly to her students. When they seemed to understand her instructions and completed their assignments, she felt she had surmounted a huge obstacle. In the early stages of culture shock, some of the "ups" can be falsely reassuring, and can actually contribute to the more intense, later stages of culture shock. Deeper issues are likely to arise—do the students find her assignments too simplistic? Or too challenging?

The "downs" are characterized by feelings of frustration and failure. Maria interpreted the disappearance of the hotel employee as an indication that she was being ignored, and in frustration repeated her story. When she saw that the employee had actually gone to find a manager with a key, she realized that she had failed to understand the signals being sent her way.

Usually culture shock occurs in predictable stages, although the duration and intensity of each stage varies among individuals. When disturbing incidents occur in the course of encounters with other cultures, people tend to blame members of the other cultures for behaving irrationally. Often, this is the result of misinterpreting the behavior of people in the other culture. Later, with a better understanding of the new culture, there is a realization that one needs to make some changes in one's own behavior in order to interact effectively.

In this early stage, Maria might assume that the employees didn't say anything because they were not fluent in English. Later, she might blame a similar occurrence on something deeper, such as a lack of training or the suspicion that they are vindictive toward foreigners. Later, around six to nine months into her stay, Maria might finally realize that she must change her own behavior to be effective in the host culture. She might have learned, for example, that a local person who says "Mmm" (like the waitress) is only

117

being politely agreeable and has not necessarily understood anything of the situation.

These experiences combine to create culture shock, which is considered a form of depression. Certain studies have also shown a physiological response, primarily within the immune system. A few people become physically ill due to culture shock, while others simply isolate themselves for several days. Some people turn inward, obsessing over their appearances or minor physical ailments. Many overindulge in food or alcohol, or sleep whenever they can as a safe route of escape from the new culture.

When recovering from culture shock, most expats are able to accept their situations, change their behavior, and gradually achieve instances of true success in the new culture. They can simultaneously view the host culture and their home culture objectively, and see positives and negatives in both. Others cannot accept change and return to their home countries earlier than planned. Some expats stay but stew and brood endlessly about the irrationality of the local culture and people.

Culture shock can be relatively mild or intense depending on a number of factors. It might be intense if a completely different language is spoken in the new location, or mild if just a different dialect of one's own language is spoken. Culture shock will certainly be intense if one does not expect to encounter differences in the new location, and milder if one expects everything to be different. It can be intense if one is relatively rigid and uninterested in learning different perspectives and trying new foods, and milder for those who are flexible, curious, and open-minded about various aspects of the new culture.

Unfortunately there is no way to avoid culture shock, although simply knowing that it will happen should lessen its intensity. Realize that it is normal. Try to maintain your sense of humor. Sleep when you feel you need it. Recognize when other people you know are suffering from it, and be nice to them. But most of all, be kind to yourself during this process of adjusting to life in Beijing.

One way to think about culture shock is to relate it to riding a roller coaster. If you anticipate each hill with dread, then you will be quite miserable as you chug your way up. If all you can think of as you begin a descent is the funny feeling you're going to have in your stomach, then it will probably feel more intense when it happens. Do your best to relax, take the hills and valleys as they come, and enjoy the ride. At your first banquet, give those sea slugs a try!

JOYS AND CHALLENGES

Over time, you will begin to see both positives and negatives about life as an expat in Beijing. While living in this marvelous city, it can be a joy to have friends and relatives from home visit you. It is nice to be able to share your new life with loved ones; their visits can alleviate homesickness, and being a tour guide can give you a sense of belonging in your new home. Early in your stay these visits can be stressful, however, as they greatly disrupt attempts to establish daily routines. Encourage people who want to visit you to do so after you have already been settled in for a few months.

Another pleasurable aspect of life in Beijing is being surrounded by an ancient and intensely interesting culture. More so than in any other Chinese city, historical monuments remind you of the past while you enjoy modern conveniences. Although violent activities during the Cultural Revolution (1966–1976) destroyed certain treasures in the city, many items that were merely damaged have been restored, and several that were destroyed or removed have been replaced with replicas. There has never been a better time to make one's home in Beijing.

The foreign community in Beijing is an extremely transient one — every day long-term foreign residents depart for their home countries; newcomers from around the world arrive in the city;

friends depart on extended home leave. This transience can be both a joy and a challenge. It is rare that other foreigners are around long enough to really get on your nerves; but just when you need to vent some frustration, you realize that your best pal has left the country for six weeks. While this can feel chaotic at the time, it also can make life in your home country seem downright sedate and boring.

Many of the challenges to living in Beijing are mentioned elsewhere in this book. Housing and the fixtures within can be of questionable quality, causing frustration or feelings of helplessness when breakdowns occur. Some days it seems like guards and government officials are everywhere, creating a sense of paranoia among expats. Despite the hoards of expats living in Beijing now, expat cliques tend to frequent a limited number of venues, making privacy downright impossible. (Expats remark that living as a foreigner in Beijing is like living in a fishbowl.) Those who have health concerns may feel that they are taking risks by staying in Beijing. Bombarded with new experiences, there is hardly time to pause and reflect, much less to find ways of sharing these experiences with family and friends back home. Keeping abreast of their news can be difficult as well.

In the end, with a few exceptions, most foreigners who have lived in Beijing say they wouldn't give up the experience for anything in the world. Despite the frustrations they faced, Beijing became home, and they would do it all over again if presented with the opportunity.

SAFETY AND SECURITY

Security is a concern in many major cities around the world, but it is not an issue of tremendous concern for expats living in Beijing. While crime exists in Beijing, the risk of expats being victims is relatively low compared with other major cities of the world. Criminals are dealt with rather quickly and strictly, and punishments can be more severe if a crime is perpetrated against a person who is not a citizen of China. Most urban housing units for expats have security personnel posted at all entrances at all times. No one gets in or out without being scrutinized.

Most women expats say that they feel quite safe in Beijing compared with other world cities. It is rare to hear talk of crimes against any expats, male or female, with the exception of being victims of petty theft or being grossly taken advantage of in bargaining sessions. Thus, women should be as cautious in Beijing as they would be in any other major world cities about keeping their handbags within view at all times, for example, but they need not worry quite as much about encountering violent crime or about walking down relatively dark streets in the evening. Outside Beijing, a higher level of vigilance is required by both men and women, as the general level of public security is lower, and foreigners are more likely to become the targets of crime.

WOMEN IN BEIJING

One of the greatest misperceptions concerning modern China has to do with the position and treatment of women in Chinese society. Perhaps the practices of foot-binding and male polygamy among the upper classes of imperial Chinese society contributed to the perception that in China, women are second-class citizens. The current reality is quite different. After the communist victory in 1949 (or as people in China say, after "liberation"), women were declared legally equal to men. This is upheld in a variety of ways in modern society, and particularly in urban Chinese societies like Beijing. As in other socialist systems, all able-bodied individuals, including women, are expected to work. Daycare has traditionally been provided by most State-owned enterprises, relieving many mothers of daytime responsibility for the care of young children. Limited mobility for China's citizens means that many people live in extended family settings; in other words, there is often at least one grandparent living in each home to assist with childcare. And the one-child policy, more strictly enforced in cities like Beijing than in the countryside, limits the amount of work necessary to care for children.

Newspapers occasionally feature articles extolling husbands who assist their wives with daily household chores. Given the importance of food in Chinese culture (see the chapter on *The Chinese Dining Experience*), most Chinese men learn to cook. In most families a man at least occasionally prepares the evening meal; some men do all the cooking for their families. This, combined with the presence in most homes of modern appliances such as washing machines, lessens the load of working women in Beijing.

Chinese women who demonstrate aptitude or possess the appropriate background for certain professions are encouraged to pursue them. Consequently, one can encounter female professionals in just about every field. Studies indicate that China has a higher percentage of women working in fields relating to science and technology than do many other industrialized nations. It is common to find women doctors, bureaucrats, and engineers working in China. However, in modern Beijing, for reasons unknown, there are at least three areas of work in which women are underrepresented: as taxi drivers, at the very top level of the national government, and at the executive level of foreign-based multinational corporations.

Women are taken seriously in business. Jokes suggesting that someone is surprised to be dealing with a female executive are not considered amusing. Women are held to the same business standards as men except, perhaps, in the area of how they are expected to entertain customers or clients. Few male business associates would expect women to stay up late at night drinking and smoking, although women are usually offered drinks and tobacco in case they would like to indulge.

Paradoxically, it is becoming a challenge for young Chinese women to get the best entry-level jobs in China. Perhaps this could be attributed to some combination of increased economic competitiveness (even among State-owned enterprises), the influence of multinationals (most of which do not provide daycare for children), the overall waning of State-provided benefits (especially for the elderly, who are living longer and sometimes require care at home), and a remaining measure of family dependence on women as primary caregivers.

Foreign women wishing to work in Beijing should not hesitate to do so. For inspiration, look to two American women, Roberta Lipson and Elyse Silverberg, who in the early 1980s started up a company to sell high-tech equipment in China. The company is still operating today, with a substantial office in Beijing and offices in a handful of other Chinese cities. In many countries around the world, it would be difficult, if not impossible, for two foreign women to start up a company and operate it successfully for 20 years. Beijing was as appropriate a setting as any for the United Nations World Conference on Women in 1995.

MATTERS OF GENDER

When it comes to physical interaction between men and women, Beijing is more relaxed than many other cities in China. Some couples, especially young ones, can be seen holding hands as they walk down the street. Young couples can also be seen hugging and smooching on park benches in the early evening hours just after it becomes dark, and sometimes even during daylight hours. One reason for this is that many young people live with extended family, and parks are one of the few types of places where couples can have some "privacy." (In Chinese cities, most people believe that they have "privacy" when they are surrounded by strangers.)

However, expats — especially non-Asian ones — should be cautious about their emotional and physical interactions with local residents. While in some cultures, flirting with and casually touching members of the opposite gender can be as normal as breathing, this is generally not true in Beijing. In Chinese thinking, even holding hands can be considered intimate behavior. Living in the backyard of the central government, people are relatively cautious about improprieties, and foreign men tend to be scrutinized more closely than are foreign women. Some foreign men have been expelled from China for being overtly aggressive in their encounters with local women. Advances that provoke a woman or her relatives to complain to authorities could result in the deportation of the foreign male in question from China.

Expat females can start rumors among local residents by being too demonstrative with men, but it is highly unlikely that complaints from local men would get the women expelled from the country. Some foreign women have been asked privately by Chinese male counterparts not to greet them too enthusiastically, particularly when they are greeted in front of the men's superiors. Keep your handshakes professional, avoid smiling too much when you greet male counterparts, and avoid other physical contact if you do not want to be the subject of rumors. As with the case for foreign men, handshakes with the other gender are fine. Tapping on the forearm is an acceptable way to get someone's attention. Foreign women should be cautious in lodging complaints about advances from local men; depending on the circumstances, the punishment for these men could be severe.

In a nutshell, it is best to avoid touching local people of the opposite gender in an affectionate way unless the two of you are romantically involved. It is acceptable for a man to extend his hand to a woman in greeting, so try to limit your physical contact to this. If you are thinking of dating a local woman, it is best if you are strongly considering a long-term relationship with her. Even your communication style can be misread. An expat who comes from a culture in which flirtation is more common, for example, might approach a Chinese woman he has been introduced to and in private say, "Oh, you are so beautiful! I hope to get to know you better." The expat might believe that this is a casual way of showing interest in a woman, whereas the Chinese woman might interpret this as, "He is interested in having a long-term relationship with me!"

Do not think that because you are just one of tens of thousands of expats working in the city that you can get away with things in Beijing. Although a tremendous number of expats resides in the city, scrutiny of interaction between expats and local people still occurs in order to prevent all concerned from getting into trouble. Anyone, married or single, who visits or resides in Beijing must deal with the realities of local perceptions concerning male-female relationships.

We have used the more inclusive term "expat," rather than foreigner, in this section because Chinese expats moving to Beijing from other countries and territories are definitely not exempt from these guidelines. Quite a large number of men of Chinese heritage go to work in Beijing, leaving their wives and children behind. Lonely, they sometimes begin relationships with local women. Unless the local women or their relatives complain, authorities cannot deal with this type of situation directly. The authorities fear the day, though, that these relationships go sour, the women and her relatives complain loudly, and the authorities might be pressured to expel the expat and put the investment of the company at risk.

At the China headquarters of one multinational, the Human Resources office began to get regular visits from government authorities responsible for foreigners. During each visit, the officials would give the Human Resources manager a copy of the rules and regulations for foreigners. It took some time for the company to realize that the authorities were hinting that the extra-marital relationship of one of the company's Chinese expat

125

executives with a local woman was known to the authorities and should be discontinued. The authorities were being indirect in order to avoid offending an investor, hoping that the company would take care of the matter internally. Expats should generally avoid romantic relationships with local people unless the expats intend to pursue long-term relationships and preferably marriage.

In another incident, an overseas Chinese man traveling with a Western woman on business was seen talking with her in the hallway of a hotel. The rooms of the man and woman were adjacent to each other, it was late in the evening, and they were seen by a hotel security guard who was walking down the hallway. He sternly motioned for the man to get back into his room. It is likely that he wasn't sure whether or not the Chinese man was local, but the security guard did not want to take any chances. The lesson from this situation is that whenever non-Chinese expats meet with Chinese people of the opposite gender, they should not be surprised by the fact that they attract attention. It is important to exercise discretion. For instance, whether in a hotel room or in a private office, they should keep the door ajar. This is a signal to everyone that nothing improper is going on behind closed doors.

This is not to say that prostitution is absent from Beijing. Foreign men staying even at five-star hotels in the city are sometimes contacted with offers of "services." Sometimes they are approached by intermediaries who lead the way to a "secret bar." There, the foreign men are confronted by people in uniforms, and are asked to pay money in order to be allowed to leave.

Prostitution has gone through periods of evanescence and resurgence over the years, so such activities should not be unexpected. However, these activities might not be based on the exact type of entrepreneurial enterprise that you imagine. Financial, political, or trade secrets have been known to land in the wrong hands after an expat has contact with prostitutes in Beijing. In other words, involvement in "joint ventures" with prostitutes could lead down commercially or physically dangerous paths. When a Western businessman was reportedly stabbed to death in his hotel room a couple of years ago in one of the rare violent crimes against foreigners occurring in Beijing, his death was ostensibly related to his involvement with a prostitute.

In China, as in many other countries in the Asia Pacific region, there is probably more physical contact among members of the same gender than with the opposite gender. It is relatively common to see two men walking down the street, the arm of one slung over the shoulders of the other, or to see two women holding hands as they talk.

Obviously, with same-gender physical contact being a bit more common than cross-gender contact in China, it is unlikely that people witnessing it will make assumptions about same-gender relationships being homosexual in nature. Actually there is very low awareness of homosexuality in China, even among most urbanites. We suggest that homosexuals keep a low profile in their personal lives and that they not divulge their sexual preferences to Chinese people, even those to whom they feel very close.

AIDS has become an issue in China, adding to governmental tension concerning extra-marital sexual relations, although unlike in some other countries, its occurrence is not widely thought of as being primarily associated with homosexual transmission.

EXPAT RELATIONSHIPS

When it comes to male-female relations among expats, authorities generally do not pay much attention. It used to be different—at one time, married couples had to produce a marriage certificate in order to stay in a hotel room together. (Couples, especially Asian or mixed-race couples, who intend to travel around China, should take with them a few copies of their marriage certificate, as producing it might still be required in places not accustomed to receiving foreign guests.) However, as with much else concerning life in Beijing, it is always wise to keep a low profile so as not to invite scrutiny.

Some issues of concern to expats living in Beijing involve dating and marital relationships. Single, non-Asian women form the group most satisfied with work life in Beijing, and yet are probably the most dissatisfied with their dating lives. For some reason, a good proportion of single expat men choose to date either local women or other Asian women who are living in Beijing. (On the whole, single men seem to have the fewest complaints about their personal lives.) It is, however, relatively rare for non-Asian females to date local men or Asian men. The combination of these tendencies greatly narrows the pool of single, available men which foreign women can date. There is no easy answer to this predicament.

For couples, some aspects of the environment in Beijing can cause severe strain on the family. Marital strain is common among expats living anywhere, as working spouses often cope with culture shock by burying themselves in what they know best—their work. Already long work hours are made even longer in Beijing by at least a couple of evening banquets a week, to which spouses are seldom invited. Dalliances between expat working men and local women, some of whom are prostitutes, are not unheard of. This can cause trouble not only with spouses, but with authorities and can lead to the transmission of serious illness as well. Non-working expat spouses can feel isolated and lonely unless they are able to establish routines of their own, make new friends, or join groups that include other non-working spouses with interests similar to theirs. Married couples should discuss this situation before moving to Beijing and perhaps try to plan how to cope. But should all else fail, some of the Western-standard medical clinics do offer counseling services.

Of course, not everyone will experience this type of relationship stress. Several dating relationships among expats that

128

started in Beijing led to marriages that continue today. Most couples find that the bonds between partners, and sometimes among all family members, are strengthened by experiencing a new culture and enduring culture shock together. Inexpensive childcare services make it relatively easy for couples to carve out quality time and reinforce their relationships.

❋ ❋ ❋

Anticipating some of the challenges you will face in Beijing will help you prepare, but a positive outlook will go even further in resolving many of the personal issues you might experience in your first year living in Beijing. Read on for some ways to keep your spirits up and your body healthy.

— CHAPTER EIGHT —

STAYING HEALTHY

Maintaining good health is an essential component of your overall well-being and your ability to withstand the waves of culture shock while living in Beijing. Serious attacks on health and sanity can come from various fronts. People who visit Beijing from other parts of the world might be surprised at the ferocity of springtime sandstorms. Although pollution levels are improving, people who have asthma or who are accustomed to relatively clear air can feel out of breath in Beijing. Stress is a common complaint of working expats, who must find ways to release the frustrations of dealing with layers of bureaucracy and to lose the weight they have gained at banquets.

DIRT AND DUST

Situated at the eastern edge of the Gobi Desert, Beijing experiences a dry climate and dusty winds. Compared with other northern cities in China, which can be among the most polluted in the world, Beijing poses an additional threat to comfort and sanity: Desert dust. Try to keep your shoes clean for an entire day in Beijing. Invariably, they take on a grayish cast that starts at the soles and works its way up. Dust "storms" can occur, usually in the early spring. Air traffic is sometimes affected by reduced visibility. Folks getting around the city complain of grit in their teeth.

So how can one cope with all this dirt and dust? Local women cope by wearing sheer mesh scarves covering their heads and faces and tied around their necks. Some people don cotton gauze masks that cover their noses and mouths. (These are also common responses to days when pollution levels in general are particularly bad.) Most foreigners just tough it out, save one accommodation: those who wear contact lenses put on their glasses instead. If you are planning a move to Beijing and you wear contact lenses, take with you a pair of eyeglasses and preferably your lens prescription as well. These days you can get fashionable eyeglasses made in Beijing for very reasonable prices.

Desert dust, together with soft coal residue in the winter, seeps into homes on a daily basis. As one expat said, "Now I know why most people hire an *ayi* to clean. It's to keep the dust down to a dull roar!" It enters your house through any tiny crevice available. Accumulations are usually visible on windowsills within hours of cleaning; hence the benefit of daily scrubbing by an energetic *ayi*. Foreigners soon learn never to walk on bare floors without shoes or sandals, as their socks or the soles of their feet quickly adopt a grayish-black hue. Carpets or the rattan "throw rugs" sold in the wicker markets are necessities for every home. They don't solve the problem, but they hide it well.

131

Expats who drive will see the Desert dust/coal residue combination in the form of a dusty black layer on their car windshields on winter mornings. The residue can be so thick that, in order to see out, the driver must turn on the windshield wipers for a moment or two before setting off. (Those who get around with the assistance of a driver are sheltered from this experience, as most Beijing drivers use feather dusters to clean their cars before starting out in the morning.)

In addition to being a nuisance, all of this dustiness and pollution can pose health challenges. Many people complain of "Beijing cough," which is also called "Beijing throat": it's a sporadic, dry cough or tickle in the throat that lasts from December through April. As far as we know, there is no way to prevent or cure "Beijing cough," aside from leaving northeast China. If you or another family member are asthmatic or have other respiratory difficulties, be sure to have a serious discussion with your physician prior to your move to Beijing.

The winter coal residue also stains. Some expats complain that their hands always look dirty. Wherever there's a fold or crevice, they're stained gray. This is common, and it takes a couple of days after leaving Beijing for the stains to go away. Light-colored shirts can also develop stains, usually along the inside of the collar and the insides of the sleeve cuffs.

Obviously, keeping one's hands dirt-free is a major challenge in Beijing. Those who live there know not to touch things like stair or escalator railings and subway hangers. In the winter, shop owners hang thick plastic, vertical strips in doorways to keep in the heat. Residents insert their hands between the slats and push the strips aside with the backs of their hands to avoid touching the strips with their palms. It's easy to identify newcomers in Beijing—they have black smudges on their faces from touching them with dusty hands. A related matter is that Chinese people are quite shocked when they see expats biting their fingernails.

Besides the fact that it does seem bizarre for people to gnaw on their own appendages, in Beijing it can contribute to your ingesting lots of dust and dirt, not to mention germs.

Although the combination of dust, pollution, and dirt is among the least attractive aspects of residence in Beijing, it should not deter you from living there. After all, there are several million Chinese people and several thousand expats coping with it every day. For most, it's just something to get used to. Conditions are likely to improve in the coming years—in preparation for the 2008 Olympics, Beijing leaders promise to engage in a major effort to build trees, plant grass, and generally improve the environment, including the quality of the air.

MEDICAL CARE

In a trend that began in the 1950s, traditional Chinese medicine departments routinely coexist with Western medicine departments in hospitals in China. And of these hospitals, Beijing sports some of the country's finest. Among them are Beijing Hospital, the central military 301 Hospital, Peking Union Hospital, and the Sino-Japanese Friendship Hospital.

Traditional Chinese medicine, to be brief, aims to develop or sustain wellness. On the other hand, Western medicine generally seeks to cure sickness. Thus Chinese medicine can often help those with illnesses considered "chronic" by practitioners of Western techniques, and certain (especially modern) diseases can be quickly quashed by Western medications. It's a wonderful mix.

Some expats are afraid of being treated at Chinese hospitals. First of all, the hospitals look unclean. Lucky we just explained the "dirt and dust" factor! It's nothing a swarm of *ayis* couldn't cure. Second, the hospitals look old. But live in Beijing for a while and you'll start to discern the pattern: wear and tear by over 10 million people can make even the best building materials look dingy pretty fast. Third, people have heard stories of less-than-rigorous use of disinfectants and sterilization techniques in Chinese hospitals and the reuse of items such as syringes that might be considered "disposable" in other countries.

There are now several Western-standard facilities available to anyone who can afford them, but the price differential with Chinese hospitals is vast. Thus, some cost-minded expats go to Chinese facilities in search of treatment for more common ailments, and to Western-standard places for inoculations, dental care, and treatment of potentially serious illnesses. Some of the Western-standard facilities available are Beijing United Family Hospital, the Beijing AEA International Clinic, and the International Medical Center. The doctors at these centers are generally Western-educated and trained. As these facilities are relatively expensive, they are most accessible to working expats and their families who are covered by employer-funded health plans. For major, non-urgent surgery, however, many foreigners still prefer the care they receive in their home countries.

A toddler attempts to climb the stairs in the lobby of Beijing United Family Hospital.

Many pregnant women used to leave Beijing for late-term care and to give birth to their children. With the opening of Beijing United Family Hospital, women began to have a local alternative. Although this facility originally specialized in practices for women and children including pediatrics, obstetrics, and gynecology, it is now a full-service hospital.

As for medical insurance, many employees and their families receive health and medical benefits through insurance policies purchased in their home countries for international coverage; by special arrangement with providers in Beijing; through self-coverage; or with a combination of these options. Medical evacuation coverage in case of extreme emergency is recommended. Ask your employer for details about coverage provided and become familiar with emergency procedures. If your company has a Human Resources department, meet the people responsible for helping during an emergency, and make sure to obtain their contact information in case you need to locate them during off hours.

MEDICINES

People who will need prescription medicines filled while living in Beijing should take with them at least one copy of each written prescription. Most prescriptions written in other countries will be accepted at pharmacies in the city, and it is best if they are written legibly in English. It is also a good idea to take along at least three months' worth of any prescription medicines until the best method of refilling them in Beijing can be determined.

To obtain prescription medicines, expats living in Beijing have several options. Many expats get prescriptions for relatively new, brand-name medicines filled at Western-style medical facilities, such as the Beijing AEA International Clinic. (Check early in your stay about the availability of medicines you will need, as some must be specially ordered from Hong Kong or other

135

locations. Certain medications might not be available in Beijing at all.) More generic and older brand-name medicines can be obtained from Chinese hospitals at a very reasonable price. Certain medicines that are available in other countries only by prescription are sometimes available over the counter at drug stores in Beijing such as Watson. Both traditional Chinese medicines and Western over-the-counter medicines (such as aspirin) can be purchased at myriad locations around the city, including some hotel gift shops and the Friendship Stores (see the chapter on *Shopping*).

HEALTH HAZARDS

Stories abound of expats encountering physical hazards in Beijing: a man, during his first day in Beijing, trips on a bit of metal pipe sticking up out of the sidewalk and falls, skinning not only his hands, but much to his embarrassment, his nose; a bicyclist rides along and suddenly finds her front tire lodged in an open manhole; a relatively tall expat nearly gets strangled by a loose stretch of telephone wire.

China certainly wants its tourists and expat guests to feel welcome. However, in the rush to modernize, issues concerning physical safety have sometimes received relatively low priority. In addition, as was mentioned in the chapter on *Finding a Home*, there is a tendency for Chinese workers to believe that *cha bu duo* (close enough) is good enough, as long as the basic purpose of any job gets accomplished. It's best to watch where you're walking in Beijing!

Other health hazards include: the water (drink it only if it has been boiled, or just drink bottled water); fresh fruits and raw vegetables (peel fruits and cook vegetables before eating); and very dry skin, especially in the winter (even the most macho men find themselves using moisturizer liberally). In addition, there are various diseases, such as hepatitis, encephalitis, and tuberculosis, to which one might not be so readily exposed at home. Ask your country's specialists on travel health, or upon arriving in Beijing, visit a medical facility accustomed to treating expats for a list of potential diseases and recommended inoculations.

Last but not least, many expats would include the habits that some Beijingers have of spitting and nose-picking on the list of health hazards. Distasteful as one might find these habits, perhaps you would agree that they deserve a relatively low ranking on this list of worries.

SMOKING

In some cities of the world, smoking has been banned in public places. Beijing is beginning to do this, but enforcement is spotty at best. Smoking is still quite popular in restaurants, although a few upscale eateries and some restaurants located in hotels have small non-smoking areas available. Some offices have also banned smoking. Theoretically, smoking is prohibited in hotel lobbies, but most hotels only enforce the ban at the reception counter, and even then not with vigor. Expats who are allergic to cigarette smoke could be quite miserable here. The only locations where "no smoking" rules are strictly enforced are temples, as many of them are made from wood and are extremely vulnerable to fire.

RESTROOMS

Some expats consider the public restroom facilities in Beijing a health hazard, although most just complain that they smell terrible. "You don't really need to look for public toilets," they say, "because you'll smell them before you can see them!" For many expats, hotels are the oases that provide relatively clean public restrooms, and they usually try to "hold it" until they can avail themselves of this service.

Either intimidated by odors or fearful of germs, there are expats who avoid using local public restrooms at all costs. A few have developed bladder or urinary tract infections as a result. Keep in mind that hundreds of thousands of Beijingers use these facilities every day with nary a blink. For expats who have trouble with the smell, momentarily breathing through the mouth might diminish the strong odor.

When you do venture to use local public restrooms, be warned that despite campaigns to improve public facilities, only the minimum in amenities is provided. Sometimes the toilet is nothing but a concrete gutter or hole in the ground over which you squat. It is unlikely that toilet paper or towels will be available, so carry a generous supply of tissues or moist disposable towels with you at all times. Newer public toilets are relatively clean, but using them costs a small fee of RMB0.20–RMB0.50.

The restroom signs in most hotels depict male and female figures to indicate the appropriate facility to use. Many local restrooms only use Chinese characters—either *nan* (man) or *nü* (woman). Refer to the *Glossary* for the appropriate Chinese character for your gender.

An additional point to note concerning restrooms is that, with the exception of hotel toilets, much of Beijing's plumbing cannot handle paper. Thus you should dispose of your used toilet paper or tissue in the wastebasket typically provided in the restroom stall. It would be quite embarrassing to be the one to cause a flash flood in a local restaurant!

STRESS BUSTERS

These days, there are plenty of outlets for stress in Beijing. Depending on the time of year, people of like interests gather to participate in activities such as swimming, throwing frisbees, practicing martial arts, or playing chess, rugby, badminton, ice hockey, or American softball.

If you enjoy jogging or hiking, you might want to join the Hash House Harriers (HHH) for their weekly jaunts on Sundays. Mind you, this group has nothing to do with drugs. There are

138

HHH groups all over Asia; they were started up by a British expat as a method of meeting others (particularly others of the opposite sex), getting some exercise, and having an opportunity to drink beer with friends. They always designate two trails: one for runners, and one for walkers. Although Hash groups can get a bit rowdy at times, some outings are held in places that expats might never visit on their own. Look for announcements of their gatherings in the *Xianzai Beijing* online newsletter and in publications geared toward expats.

Many hotels in Beijing have health clubs which long-term expat residents are usually encouraged to join whether or not they live in the hotel complex. The fitness center at the Swissôtel, for example, has all the latest equipment and a full-time manager. Beijing even has golf courses, but the fees are steep.

Expats who desire to venture closer to the local culture might visit the parks of Beijing in the early morning to observe people — mostly senior citizens — practicing calisthenics, ballroom dancing, *taijiquan* (the ancient art of Chinese shadow boxing), or *qigong* (exercises which require deep breathing and concentration). If you want to join in, you must distinguish yourself from the tourists who come only to gawk. Show up every morning, and stay for the duration. After a few days, you will most likely be invited to join in; perhaps you will be taught *taijiquan* or *qigong* by a true master!

Parks are a favorite gathering spot for morning exercises.

139

Getting a massage is another popular way to reduce stress. China is famous for its blind massage masters, and massages are relatively inexpensive and available at most hotels. There are also professional masseurs and masseuses who make house calls; some expats schedule weekly appointments. Of course, it is cheaper if you can find a good non-hotel massage parlor to visit, but the masseurs and masseuses there are not likely to speak English nor to be accustomed to working with expats. Ask long-time residents for their recommendations concerning massages. For a truly local experience, try the massage masters who set up their cots outdoors along the outer edges of parks.

All this said, the most common way that expats relieve stress in Beijing is by meeting at restaurants for a few drinks and dinner with friends. The local culture rubs off on you!

❊❊❊

Some tips to remember when preparing to move to Beijing:
- take eyeglasses and/or lens prescriptions with you
- talk to your doctor if you have respiratory problems
- get recommended inoculations
- bring along at least three months' supply of prescription medicines

A park-side Beijing massage center.

— CHAPTER NINE —

THE CHINESE DINING EXPERIENCE

The people of China take great pride and pleasure in their cuisine. While living in Beijing, you will have many opportunities to dine on authentic Chinese cuisine in its native setting. Beijing has its own distinctive style of cooking—perhaps best represented by the world-famous "Peking duck." Because Beijing is the capital of China, cuisines from practically every region of the country (such as Guangdong, Shanghai, and Sichuan), as well as Muslim and vegetarian cuisines, can be found somewhere in the metropolis. While you are living in Beijing, make the most of your stay. Try a type of Chinese cooking that you have not tried before. Be adventurous!

141

Examples of Regional Cuisines of China and their Basic Characteristics	
Beijing	oily; dark sauces; use of vinegar
Guangdong (Cantonese)	mild, light sauces; fresh ingredients
Shanghai	slightly sweet sauces; preserved ingredients
Sichuan	spicy; aromatic

SHARING MEALS

Chinese people consider their cuisine to be a central component of Chinese culture. Friends and colleagues will inevitably invite you to share meals with them, as they consider this an indispensible part of showing hospitality and building relationships. Some expats involved in commercial endeavors find the frequency of formal Chinese dinners, or "banquets," overwhelming. (See the chapter on *Working in Beijing* for more information on banquets.)

When there are more than four or five people sharing a meal, Chinese diners prefer sitting at a round table. This makes it easier to talk and interact with each other, and to build the relationships necessary to function in Chinese society. These occasions can be quite lively and noisy. Particularly if you are just visiting or have recently arrived in Beijing, Chinese people are likely to consider themselves the "hosts" and you the "guest," no matter who is officially hosting (or paying) for the meal. Chinese people are enormously proud of their food and want to share this "jewel," or perhaps more appropriately the "pearl," of their culture with you. Try not to disappoint your Chinese hosts by turning down an invitation to share a meal. Accepting the invitation and demonstrating appreciation for Chinese cuisine will get your relationship off to a good start.

DINING OUT

With a pained look on his face, an expat said, "I've been living in Beijing for a couple of years now, but no one has ever invited me home for dinner. What am I doing wrong?" The answer: nothing. Chinese people rarely host other Chinese people in their homes, much less expats.

When Chinese people invite guests to share a meal, they almost always plan to meet in a restaurant. There are various reasons for this. One reason is that Chinese food is meant to be served as soon as it is cooked. Few Chinese homes have ovens, and even if they did, it would be inappropriate to keep one dish warm while others are being prepared. Thus the "chef" cannot sit down to eat and chat until every dish has been cooked and served.

Another reason for dining out is a preference for quantity and variety in terms of the food served to guests. The rule of thumb is that a host should provide at least one dish per person at a table, which all guests then share; the larger the variety the better. If only two to three people share a meal, there are at most three or four dishes to try. On the other hand, if a Chinese host can assemble a group of eight people or more (12 is usually the maximum per table), then guests will be able to taste a great variety of dishes.

Chinese homes also tend to be too small to comfortably accommodate large numbers of guests. The overall tendency of Chinese people to dine out in large groups leads many expats to call even relatively informal Chinese meals "banquets."

ORDERING FOOD

Surprising to many expats is the amount of conversation involved in the process of ordering a Chinese meal. After diners have been seated in a restaurant, usually within just a few moments, a server appears, hands each person a menu, and stands with pen poised and order form in hand. (Actually, this happens mostly at local restaurants. Servers at hotel restaurants catering to foreigners have

143

been trained to leave the table for a few minutes while the customers read their menus.) No matter how long it takes to read the menu and decide what to order, the server does not leave! It is the server's job to wait beside the table and discuss details about the food. At this point, a Chinese host might ask guests if they would prefer to order any dishes in particular. If you find yourself in this situation, please decline. Absolutely do not say, "Oh, sure, I'd love some sweet and sour pork!" The host is merely demonstrating graciousness in asking about your preferences. Instead, say something like, "I'm sure you know which dishes are best at this restaurant." However, if you have any food allergies or other dietary restrictions, this would be an appropriate time to mention them.

When Chinese people go to a restaurant for the first time, they usually ask what unique dishes the restaurant is known for, and what the specials of the day are. They might make some small talk, perhaps starting with a remark about how busy the restaurant is. They will ask further questions about menu items they don't recognize, and will ask which vegetables and meat are freshest.

Here is a sample of a conversation between a Chinese host and the server:

Diner:	*Ni hao.*
Server:	*Ni hao.*
Diner:	(long pause as the diner peruses the menu) *So what do you have tonight that is particularly good?*
Server:	*Well, our house specialty is braised pork cubes.*
Diner:	*Is it good?*
Server:	*Very delicious. But your foreign guests probably won't like it. It's rather fatty.*
Diner:	*Mmmm...What kind of vegetables do you have tonight?*
Server:	*We have spinach, pea leaves with garlic, and broccoli.*

Diner:	*Can we get the pea leaves without garlic? We want to order the garlic sliced beef, and together it might be too much garlic.*
Server:	*Sure, that's OK.*
Diner:	*We have the pea leaves and garlic sliced beef so far. Are there any other dishes you would recommend?*
Server:	*Some of our guests enjoy the chicken and tofu in black bean sauce.*
Diner:	*No, that doesn't sound very good. How about your roast duck. Is that any good?*
Server:	*Which one?* (leans over to look at the menu)
Diner:	*This one.*
Server:	*Many people order it, but I've never had it.*
Diner:	*Well, let's try it.*
Server:	*OK. You have a total of three dishes now. Don't you want some fish? Our carp is very good.*
Diner:	*No, I don't think so, we're not that hungry.*
Server:	*What about soup? Both the winter melon soup and our hot and sour soup are delicious.*
Diner:	*The winter melon soup sounds good. We'll have that...*

This conversation could go on for several more minutes; often the ordering process takes 10 minutes or so. The more diners there are in a group, the longer it will take because more dishes must be ordered. While you are witnessing an interaction of this type, please be patient. Some expats start looking around the room or tapping the table impatiently, but it is important to act interested in the process even though you might not understand much of what is being said. Your level of interest will indicate to others your level of "civilization."

Notice that, in the scenario above, the server and diner both say *Ni hao* (How are you?) to each other. Some foreigners—

including Chinese people who are not originally from Beijing—do not have the habit of greeting service staff, but this is almost always done in Beijing. Be sure to say *Ni hao* when you begin transactions with any service providers, including restaurant servers, taxi drivers, and store staff.

Ordering food is generally the responsibility of the host and is best done by a Chinese person. Chinese meals are supposed to contain a balance of sauces (light and dark), flavors (salty and sweet), textures (crunchy and soft), and ingredients (only one or two dishes made from each main ingredient, such as beef or tofu). The complexity involved in achieving this balance extends the time it takes to order a meal, especially when ordering for a large group of people (the greater the number of dishes to be ordered, the greater the challenge in achieving balance). It is rare to find expats who have the skills necessary for ordering meals to the satisfaction of Chinese guests.

If you must host a meal alone or with other expats (in other words, if you do not have any Chinese people as members of the host party to order the food), try to order the dishes in advance with the assistance of a Chinese person. If this is not possible, then it is acceptable to ask the most senior Chinese person in the guest party to do the ordering for you. Naturally this person will refuse the honor a couple of times, because asking guests what they would like to eat is a typical gesture of a Chinese host. Explain that ordering Chinese food is too complicated for you and again ask for the person's assistance. Once the person is sure that you are sincere, then he or she will happily make the appropriate selections. After all, it will ensure the Chinese people at the table of a balanced meal that they can savor.

DINING ETIQUETTE

Unlike Western dining etiquette, Chinese etiquette does not involve too many rules about physical behavior, such as where you should put your elbows or hands while you are eating. Instead, most of the "rules" concern hosts and guests acting appropriately in their respective roles. This behavior can vary, however, based on how close the relationships are among hosts and guests, and the degree of formality of the occasion.

It is the host's obligation to take care of guests. When you are the principal host, you should be at the restaurant before your guests so that you can greet everyone as they arrive. Ask the principal guest to sit in the seat of honor, which some experts say is the seat with its back to the wall and farthest from the door. Other experts say that it is the next seat to the right. In either case, when sitting down, your seat as the principal host is the first seat to the left of the principal guest. (This way you can easily serve food to the principal guest using your right hand.) The interpreter, if one is present, sits in the first seat to the right of the principal guest.

Particularly at the beginning of the meal, each member of the host party should be sure that the guests' plates and glasses are never empty. Even if guests "protest," hosts should serve them anyway, as the "protests" are meant to be gestures of modesty. After the first course or two has been served, many hosts invite guests to serve themselves for the remainder of the meal. If this is a formal banquet, the principal host should offer a toast with expressions of goodwill and friendship to the principal guest or to all members of the guest party. Usually this is done after one of the early courses has been put on the table, but before food is put on the guests' plates. At the end of the meal, hosts should thank the guests for coming and personally say goodbye to them.

When you are a "guest," it is your role to show appreciation and gratitude to your host(s). As the host is supposed to arrive at the restaurant first, don't go in if you see that the host is not there yet! It would be an embarrassment (or loss of face) for the host. Instead, come back when you are sure the host has arrived. Even if you know that you are the principal guest, when you are invited to take the seat of honor, you should politely decline once or twice before finally accepting the honor. Likewise, when members of the host party put food on your plate and fill your glass, thank them and protest, saying that you can serve yourself. (Try to put food on their plates, too, once in a while.)

If the host has offered you a toast, then you should offer a return toast after the next course is presented. During meals, Chinese hosts will often "apologize" for the poor quality or limited quantity of the food, even when both are exceptional. The proper responses are to praise both. After fruit or dessert has been served and as soon as everyone has finished eating, you should thank the host. Mention what a wonderful meal it was and how much you enjoyed the occasion.

Once everyone stands up from the table, neither hosts nor guests linger to chat. They depart immediately. What needs to be said should have been said while everyone was sitting around the table. It seems as though banquet participants get sucked out of the restaurant by a vacuum cleaner once the meal is over!

By the way, perhaps we should mention that there are a few Chinese dining rules concerning physical behavior. Don't point or gesture with your chopsticks, or stick them vertically in your rice bowl. And please don't flavor your rice with soy sauce or gravy—only children do that. When you serve yourself from a central serving dish, take pieces of food only from whichever side of the plate is nearest to you, even if the pieces are bigger or smaller than you really would like. The size of the serving that you take should only be one or two modest spoonfuls; wait until everyone else at the table has had the opportunity to take some of the dish before taking seconds.

Speaking of the serving dishes, do not lift them from the table. Just reach across the table to get some food and put it on your plate, or move your plate toward the serving dishes. In one situation, a newly arrived expat announced, "Well, if no one wants any more of the shrimp, I'll finish it!" With that, he hoisted the serving dish and scraped the remainder onto his plate. His hosts appreciated his relish for the food but were aghast at how he demonstrated it.

Actually, this energetic diner violated two points of etiquette in one fell swoop. Not only are diners not supposed to lift the serving dishes, but according to traditional Chinese custom, leaving at least a small amount of food on one's plate and on each serving dish is an indication that the guests had plenty to eat. In recent years, with the growing affluence in Beijing, so much food is left over at banquets that guests are routinely given "doggy bags" full of leftovers to take home.

In general, take your cue from the Chinese at the table as to what is acceptable dining behavior. Some customs that foreigners might find awkward, but which are generally accepted in Chinese dining, include bringing one's head and shoulders toward the table and lifting the rice bowl with one hand (except in very formal settings). This makes it much easier to eat rice with chopsticks!

PAYING THE BILL

In reality, everyone pretty much knows whose turn it is to pay. Gestures of friendship should be reciprocated. Therefore, if a Chinese friend or colleague has hosted a meal, you must do your best to host the next one. Chinese people keep a fairly accurate mental calculation of how many meals each person, couple, or group has hosted.

At the end of informal meals (not banquets) shared by only a few people, you will often witness Chinese people "fighting" over who will pay for the meal. For example, you might observe them trying to grab the check from the server, or from one of the other diners. Hosting a meal is a sign of hospitality and a gesture of friendship and goodwill, not to mention being an issue of "face."

It should be noted that young people, much to the dismay of their more traditionally-minded parents, bosses, or teachers, will often split the bill among friends rather than expecting one individual to pay each time.

CHOOSING RESTAURANTS

Chinese Food

There are generally three types of Chinese restaurants found in Beijing. The first type is found in hotels, and is relatively expensive and formal. This is where foreign visitors and expats often choose to eat Chinese food, as the menus and staff are bilingual, the service is good, and the plates and utensils are generally clean. Many have a theme of some sort of regional Chinese cooking. The restaurant at the top of the Great Wall Sheraton promotes Sichuan cuisine, for example, and the China Garden Restaurant at the Holiday Inn Lido Beijing offers Cantonese fare. Expats who don't speak Mandarin can confidently entertain Chinese guests at these restaurants, as they can order more easily and will have a better-than-average chance of actually getting and paying the bill. Added to these other conveniences is the fact that customers can almost always pay by credit card.

The second type of restaurant includes both State-owned as well as private non-hotel eateries. These tend to be darker, smokier, and noisier than the hotel establishments. Ordering can be challenging as most menus are in Chinese only. You can pay by credit card at some, but most operate on a cash-only basis. Prices for a dinner for two vary widely, from about RMB100 (US$12) up to the sky-high cost of such a dinner in any world capital. A cautionary note is that service in State-owned restaurants can still have the surly edge of what passed for service in the early 1980s.

If you do not speak Mandarin well and cannot read Chinese characters, one way to order food in local restaurants is to ask the staff about dishes that people at nearby tables are eating. Other methods are learning to pronounce the names of your favorite Chinese dishes, or asking someone to write them out in Chinese characters. Most restaurants have their own special dishes but can also make just about any typical dish you may want to order.

Finally, local food stalls situated near bustling shopping areas and markets are available for extremely casual dining. Some expats are wary of the standards of refrigeration, food preparation, and cleanliness, and avoid participating in this experience. Some expats on limited budgets, such as students, swear they've had their best meals at these places.

Foreign Food

When you are longing for tastes from your home country, or want to linger at your table long after you've finished eating dinner, you can choose to dine at a Western or other non-Chinese restaurant. Many of the best restaurants for fine dining are found in hotels. Try Justine's at the Jianguo Hotel for French food or Goninbyakusho at the Beijing Hotel for Japanese food.

A Chinese open-air food stall in Beijing serves lunch.

151

Hotel coffee shops are pretty standard, and serve food prepared with mostly imported ingredients. Of course, some of these ingredients are "exported" from Guangdong Province to Hong Kong, and then sold as "imported" to buyers in northern China. But, never mind. Once you're a resident of Beijing, you'll probably choose hotel restaurants only when you are entertaining Chinese guests, when you are arranging to meet short-term visitors to Beijing (the hotels are easiest for neophytes to find), when it's really hot and you need the relief of reliable air-conditioning, or when you entertain fussy foreign visitors who come to stay with you in Beijing.

Otherwise, most foreign residents of Beijing get together at the "joint venture independent" restaurants ("joint venture" because the team that owns it must include at least one local resident and one foreign resident; "independent" because the restaurant is not affiliated with a hotel). Many of these opened up in the early 1990s, and fashion food for the foreign palate from locally available ingredients. The two most well-known of these are Frank's Place (near the Worker's Stadium) and Schiller's Pub (the original one, across from the Kempinski Hotel); both serve Western-style pub food. There are many other types of cuisine available at "joint venture independent" restaurants: try the Metro Café near the Workers' Stadium for Italian food, Phrik Thai for the cuisine of Thailand, the Golden Elephant for Indian food, or the Mexican Wave for Mexican food. Several of these restaurants have outdoor seating in the summer, providing relief from the indoor haze of cigarette smoke. Watch out for hungry mosquitoes, though.

A final, general word on dining concerns the practice of tipping. As mentioned previously in the section on taxi drivers, there is officially no tipping in China. Many of the restaurants located in hotels charge a service fee of 15%. In local Chinese restaurants, the staff isn't likely to know what to do with a tip, so don't leave one. It is possible but completely optional to leave a small tip when dining in some of the "joint venture independent" restaurants—the tips are usually pooled and then distributed among the serving staff.

❉ ❉ ❉

Although a few restaurants have been recommended here, they are perhaps more susceptible than any other type of location to overnight disappearance. An expat recently commented, "Some of these restaurants in Beijing have been reborn more than Buddha." Please forgive us if any of them are in their next life by the time you go looking for them!

The widespread availability of great food is one of the most pleasurable aspects of living in Beijing these days. And the more you seem to enjoy Chinese food, the more comfortable your new friends and colleagues will feel in your presence.

For French cuisine, visit Justine's at the Jianguo Hotel.

153

Chapter Ten

SHOPPING

Shopping in Beijing used to be more aggravating than interesting. These days the variety of options for browsing and buying is likely to make newcomers feel dizzy. There are many different types of stores in which to buy all kinds of products, but only some sell the imported goods that are popular among expats. Product availability can swing wildly, contributing to expat frustration. In some locations, such as markets, bargaining is a time-consuming must. The solution to many of these shopping issues is to choose with care the places in which you shop and the goods you buy in each locale.

SHOPPING OPTIONS

Toward the end of the 1970s and into the very early 1980s, most stores in China were State-owned. Now, while many smaller shops are privately owned, most larger stores remain State-owned. Several of the larger stores along Wangfujing (the most famous shopping street in Beijing), for example, are State-owned, and so are the Friendship Stores. Newcomers tend to prefer shopping in these stores, as the goods for sale range from average to better-than-average quality, and the arts and crafts are usually genuine. Prices are as marked—there is no bargaining except on large quantity or big-ticket purchases—and vary little from store to store.

As for the concept of the Friendship Store, this is a unique institution of China found in many of its major cities. Originally there were only two in Beijing, both conveniently located in the neighborhoods frequented by foreign diplomats and journalists. As you might guess from having read the *Welcome to Beijing* chapter, one was in Jianguomenwai and the other was in Sanlitun. Both of these stores still exist today. The cachet of these shops was that they were pretty much the only places in town to purchase imported foodstuffs, liquor, and cigarettes. All purchases had to be made in FEC. In addition, the Jianguomenwai store offered a relatively large selection of other imported items for sale, such as Kodak film and the *International Herald Tribune* newspaper, as well as export-quality Chinese goods such as souvenirs and clothing. In essence, the Friendship Stores allowed China to manage its foreign currency balance right down to the consumer level. Until the mid-1980s, the average Chinese person wasn't even allowed in the front door of these stores, and purchases could not be transacted in *renminbi*.

When the Jianguo Hotel opened, it contained a small gift shop or *xiaomaibu* (literally, "department for small sales"). There one could purchase the international editions of foreign magazines, foreign-language newspapers, imported cigarettes, and rather pricey souvenirs. The *xiaomaibu* in a few other hotels followed suit. Again, one needed FEC to purchase these items, and Chinese people weren't allowed into hotels where foreign visitors stayed unless they could prove the legitimacy of their visits.

Around this time (the early to mid-1980s), China began allowing individuals and farmers to privately sell produce and snacks in specially designated areas of Beijing called "free markets." The quality and quantity of produce rose some, but were still limited given Beijing's harsh winters. Later, the concept of the free market was extended to clothing and household goods.

As the free markets loosened the local economy, entrepreneurs were also allowed to open small owner-operated stores in various parts of the city. An interesting pattern can be noticed in the free markets and these pockets of individual entrepreneurship in Beijing, as well as in other Chinese communities around the world — vendors of similar goods tend to be huddled together. Thus vegetable markets constitute rows and rows of shops selling essentially the same produce, and certain stretches of city streets sell kitchen utensils, for example, or automobile paraphernalia.

A possible explanation for this bunching together of like vendors is, "so that customers will know where to go." In other words, if customers want certain items, they will know which street or neighborhood they should visit. There is a certain status conveyed on vendors by having their shops in neighborhoods of like vendors — customers tend to believe that in order to be located there, the vendors must be reputable. Furthermore, as business directories or "yellow pages" in Beijing usually do not include very small shops, customers must ask friends and family who is the best vendor from which to buy certain goods. (In other words, without a personal referral, it is rare for Chinese people to shop in a small store run by a complete stranger.) Thus, for vendors, being situated right next to their competitors really has little impact on customer flow. Yet another theory is that individual vendors might use their physical proximity to band together and get volume discounts on wholesale purchases.

Today, many people shop for produce, snacks, and clothing in the free markets and at small stores dotting Beijing. Goods for sale now come from all over China, so there's plenty of variety. Little bargaining goes on with snack vendors, but shoppers bargain freely with produce and clothing vendors.

The opening of the China World Trade complex at the end of 1986 brought the modern mall to Beijing, complete with multiple levels of upscale stores and coffee shops. These days there are several glitzy, upscale malls to choose from, like the Vantone New World and Oriental Plaza. Many include outlets of foreign supermarket chains that offer imported as well as domestic goods, such as the Park 'n' Shop outlet in the basement of Full Link Plaza (Chaoyang).

With all these options—State-owned stores, hotel gift shops, free markets, small shops, and malls—it is possible to enjoy a wide array of shopping experiences in modern Beijing. The challenge for a newcomer is making this variety work for you, rather than against you. After you've lived in Beijing for a while, you will find yourself making shopping choices based on a much wider set of criteria than before. A likely determinant will be how much time you have to devote to shopping—depending on which culture you're from, you might not be used to allocating time for the bargaining required in the markets. (To save themselves time, some people have their *ayi* do the daily shopping in the markets for vegetables and fruit. See the *Getting Settled* chapter for details on employing an *ayi*.)

Another determinant is the availability of more than one type of good. Local grocery stores tend to carry all Chinese-made goods, whereas places like Park 'n' Shop carry imported products as well.

157

Some expats feel that paying higher prices for vegetables at Park 'n' Shop is worth the money, because unlike in local stores, they can buy all the other things they need at the same time, with the added benefit of not having to bargain.

The most recent additions to the Beijing shopping scene are the hypermarket chains. These include internationally known chains such as Carrefour and Price Club. Other warehouse stores and supermarkets like PriceSmart, Jian (this is the name as it is spelled on its signs, although the Chinese name is Huapu), CTA Makro, and Wang Jing offer easy shopping and value for money. Certain hypermarkets are available to members only, some lean toward bulk or volume sales, and others are simply large supermarkets. Carrefour carries a number of imported French foodstuffs unavailable elsewhere and has an excellent and affordable wine selection. Note that none of these places is for the faint of heart or claustrophobic, especially on weekends and holidays. CTA Makro doesn't admit small children, and shoppers

The street outside a Chinese department store is a busy place.

must bring their own bags to carry out their purchases. A number of foreign suppliers of home furnishings such as Ikea have also set up shop in Beijing.

MARKETS

Produce and Meat

In the 1980s and before, most people in Beijing survived on food that was grown locally. Given the cold winters and sandy, not-so-fertile soil, the selection of fresh produce was basically limited to watermelon in the summer and cabbage in the fall. Now not only are local farmers growing a wider variety of produce, but improved infrastructure means more goods grown in warmer southern China can be purchased in northern markets.

Local markets remain the best places to get fresh vegetables and fruit at reasonable prices, despite the convenience of supermarkets. Agricultural methods used in China, however, dictate that special care be taken when preparing produce bought either in supermarkets or local markets. One of the most widely used fertilizers in China is human excrement, also sometimes referred to as "night soil." Although some expats in Beijing wash their fresh vegetables in diluted bleach in order to eat them raw, this is not recommended as a daily, long-term practice. All vegetables should be peeled (if possible) and cooked to prevent the transmission of diseases. Also, certain pesticides that have been banned in other countries are still used in China, especially on hanging fruit like grapes and apples, so it is imperative to eat only the flesh of the fruit and to discard the peels.

As for meat, there is a wide variety available in Beijing. Given the sizeable Muslim population, one can even find *halal* (prepared according to Muslim tradition) meat vendors throughout the city. It is recommended that expats avoid purchasing meat in local markets, as most vendors have no refrigeration available. Instead,

159

most expats purchase meat in the supermarkets or from specialty shops. One of the oldest and most popular spots for purchasing meat is what among expats is informally called the "German Butcher" (the Chinese name is the Hua'an Meat Store). This shop was formerly located in Sanlitun and has been moved to a site near Chaoyang Park. Expats venture to Beijing from other cities in China, such as Tianjin, to shop at the German Butcher because they believe the store maintains better sanitary conditions than most local vendors, along with offering nice homemade, German-style sausages.

Durable Goods

Some of the durable goods markets, especially those selling clothing, are oriented more toward tourists than local residents. The best advice anyone could give you in terms of shopping in these markets is, "buyer beware." Some branded articles are genuine factory overruns, but a substantial portion of the branded items available in clothing markets is counterfeit, and the residents of some countries could have their purchases confiscated if they attempt to take them home. Many of the furniture and antique markets, such as Panjiayuan (known to foreigners as the "dirt market"), contain a certain amount of new items intentionally altered to look old.

In the durable goods markets, more so than in the produce markets, buying can be a group experience. When workers at a booth sense that they have a real buyer on their hands, they are likely to gather around to help a colleague successfully complete a sale. When the buyer is an expat or foreign visitor, other shoppers crowd around to see precisely what it is that the buyer would be interested in purchasing. (Chinese people are in general curious about human activity, whether it's a bus accident or just a foreign visitor buying something. As one Chinese person explained, "We have little control over events in our lives. Going to see what other people are doing is something over which we have complete control.") Because of this tendency, it is best for foreign buyers not to linger too long over products that they do not plan to purchase. Those who have found an item that they want to buy should just relax and enjoy being the center of attention for a while.

Speaking of durable goods, taking up residence in Beijing means you will occasionally need things like cooking utensils and perhaps even appliances. For small hardware, pots, pans, and kitchen gadgets, the prices you can negotiate at the local markets and small Chinese shops can't be beat. Chinese department stores also have a pretty good selection of appliances made in China under a variety of local and foreign brand names. But for more reasonably priced used appliances, get yourself connected to the word-of-mouth network among expats. When expat families prepare to leave Beijing, they often sell most of their appliances and sometimes furniture as well, at a reduced price rather than taking them home — especially if they bought electrical appliances locally and the voltage doesn't match the voltage back home.

SHOPPING CHALLENGES

Shoppers in Beijing face several challenges. Getting to more than a couple of stores can take the better part of the day. Beijing is spread out, and stores selling items that expats want to buy are not all located together. Extra time often needs to be budgeted for the shopping experience.

The best overall shopping for expats is in the East City and Chaoyang Districts, as they are the sites of the greatest number of stores carrying goods that expats want to purchase. If you live in one of these neighborhoods but don't have a car, shopping can be manageable via bicycle. Otherwise, you will always have to add the cost of taxis to the total expense of any goods you buy. Taxi fares add up, because it's rare to be able to find everything one needs at any single store. Keep this in mind when deciding in

161

which neighborhood to live in Beijing.

Many expats complain that communicating with store staff can be a chore. Although certain types of stores (especially ones that cater to tourists or are foreign-owned) hire workers who have some foreign language abilities, most shopkeepers and store employees speak no foreign languages with the exception of some rudimentary English. This is a great reason to start your lessons in Mandarin early and keep at them.

Another challenge for shoppers in Beijing is the notion of service, or the lack thereof. Things have improved immensely over the past two decades, but a lackadaisical attitude is still more frequently encountered in Beijing than in other cities such as Guangzhou or Shanghai. Part of the explanation could be that northerners just tend to move more slowly and in general, show less emotion than do southerners. A specific trait of Beijing work culture, though, is that management tends to be more focused on political correctness than on teaching subordinates savvy service techniques. Whatever the reasons, it is important to not lose patience. Although in south China, expressing impatience is an acceptable tactic for getting the attention of service providers, it always backfires in Beijing. Trust us. Cajoling works much better.

Over the years, an enduring and frustrating aspect of shopping in Beijing has been that sometimes it is impossible to find a certain type of product. One month, it's scouring powder that is missing from every store you enter. The next month, it's chocolate chips. In these instances, expats go around the city asking each other, "Got any (such-and-so)?" Anyone who has extra would be a cad not to share it with others. And, for some products such as wine, expats pay dearly whether buying it at a private shop or in a restaurant, because import duties are levied to protect local production. For both reasons, expats leave Beijing with empty luggage in order to stock up on precious items during trips home.

At first, newcomers tend to buy imported goods because they

don't know what domestic substitutions are available, but eventually they replace imported goods with local products. This can drastically reduce food bills. In some cases, expats find that they like some Chinese products better than the imports. Perhaps, for example, they find Chinese peanuts preferable to American ones — Chinese peanuts are generally sweeter than American peanuts and have less aftertaste. Some expats have teamed with local merchants or formed joint ventures to produce goods, such as organic vegetables, that these expats know other expats would want to buy. Ultimately, most expats go to Chinese stores for half of their shopping and to foreign-owned stores for the rest. This method of shopping is relatively economical but takes time.

BARGAINING

Most Chinese people prefer to bargain for what they buy. They feel they get the best possible price, and bargaining is something over which they have some control. In the eyes of Chinese people, the bargaining process is also the fine art of forming and maintaining a relationship with a vendor. It is like playing a game of chess with a worthy partner or rival, sparring with good humor while getting to know the other person better. Although it is often said that Chinese people are great negotiators, in reality, they are not good strategic planners. However, they learn solid bargaining tactics starting at a young age.

An important preparatory step in bargaining is to determine a fair price for whatever you want to buy. For durable goods, go to the Friendship Store or another fixed-price shop to guage prices and investigate what constitutes good quality. (With items such as antiques, jade, or pearls, it might take extra research, time, and experience to really understand the quality issues involved.) Another preparatory step is to pay a couple of preview visits to a market without buying anything, to see which vendor seems to have the best products and seems to have the most regular

163

customers. Probably that vendor treats regular customers well. Before you are ready to buy, begin to establish a relationship with the vendor. Chat a bit each time you go, or as much as you can given that most independent shop owners speak little English.

Once you've found a suitable vendor and you've decided on something you want to buy in that vendor's booth or shop, it's important to appear interested in two or three items that the vendor has for sale. It's likely to drive up the price if the vendor sees you returning to the booth more than once and looking at only one item. In other words, if the vendor senses that you are already set on one item in particular and is able to identify which one, the price goes up accordingly.

The first tactic to use in your actual bargaining transaction with a vendor should be to establish yourself as a local resident. (For example, when asked where you are from, proudly say, "Beijing!" with a smile. If you are a native speaker of Chinese but are not from Beijing, try to use the local dialect or some local vocabulary appropriately in at least your first few utterances.) If you convey the impression that you are a long-term resident of the city, either through words or actions, you will almost always get a better price for what you buy. Conversely, if vendors sense that you are not from Beijing, they might try to gouge you on price or give you the poorest quality items they have. After all, if you're leaving tomorrow, it's a one-time transaction and is unlikely to affect either the vendor's reputation or repeat business.

However, just by mentioning or demonstrating that you are a resident of Beijing does not mean that you will get as low a price as a local person. Japanese people tend to get quoted the highest prices, followed by people who look Western, and then by people with darker skin, such as those from Pakistan or Nigeria. Other Asians qualify for the next lower prices, while people from Beijing or other parts of China are generally given the best deals. Of course, the better your relationship with the vendor, the lower the price, and price differences will be directly related to the prices of the items. In other words, if you are a foreigner, it is probably not worth bargaining for an hour to get five *fen* (cents) off the price of vegetables just to try to get a more "local" price. However, foreigners might want to send Chinese people to bargain on their behalf for big-ticket items.

The manner in which people bargain does not vary much. Ask how much an item costs. No matter what price the vendor quotes, repeat whatever price you heard and say, "Too expensive!" (*Tai gui!*) Repeating the price serves to confirm that you heard it correctly. Some buyers enact this step with a good dose of drama, showing surprise to underline how shocked they are or looking chagrined to indicate that they would never be able to afford the object at such a high price. The next move on price is yours; you are expected to state an offer. Generally, in Beijing, your offer can be about 30–50% off the price quoted to you. A better guideline is that your offer should be 15–20% less than you intend to pay for the item. Also, if you make an offer at this stage, you should be sincere about wanting to buy if the vendor eventually gives you a reasonable price. If you are not sincere, walk away. To waste the vendor's time for your own amusement is to ensure sky-high prices when you visit this or any other vendor in the same market in the future, as word of your insincerity will spread quickly.

Gradually work your way toward a compromise price. It's not necessary to make concessions each time the ball is in your court. In fact, you should stick with your offer for one or two rounds, while weaving in some amiable conversation. The following conversation is an example of the process. Let's say that the buyer speaks Chinese, is interested in purchasing an old chair at an antiques market, and has already done research on quality and prices.

Buyer: *Ni hao.*

Seller: *Ni hao. Welcome!*

Buyer: *How much for the chair?*

Seller: *That chair? How much do you want to pay?*

Buyer: *Well, I don't know really. How much is it?*

Seller: *For you, 640 kuai.*

Buyer: (Eyes wide with surprise) *640 kuai!* (Shaking head from side to side) *I didn't realize these were so expensive.*

Seller: *How much do you want to pay?*

Buyer: *Well, I don't know. My friends here in Beijing told me I could find chairs like this for about 300 kuai.*

Seller: *Ah, you live in Beijing?*

Buyer: *Yes, we moved here two months ago. My husband works for Siemens. Do you know that company?*

Seller: *It's a German company, right?*

Buyer: *That's right. And, it's a big company. So if you give me a good price, I can tell my husband's colleagues to come here and buy from you.*

Seller: *We have very good quality items.*

Buyer: *Yes, well, how about 320 kuai for that chair.*

Seller: *320 kuai?* (Feigning outrage...) *That's less than the cost of the chair!* (...then becoming animated) *We are known for our top quality! This is an excellent chair. Sit in it! Sit!* (Buyer sits in chair) *You see how nice it is? It's very sturdy. Besides, it's very old.*

Buyer: *How old?*

Seller: *Well, I don't know, probably at least 100 years old. It's a Qing Dynasty antique! You pay 580 kuai, OK?*

Buyer: *580 kuai? That's still too much. My husband will be angry with me for spending so much. What about that other chair? How much is that?*

Seller: *If you buy both, I will give them to you for 1,060, or 530 kuai for each one. OK?*

Buyer: *How can I buy two chairs if I can't afford the first one? Maybe I can pay 375 kuai for just one.*

Seller: *Your husband works for Siemens. I think you're very rich; it's no problem. 530 kuai each for two chairs is a very good price.*

Buyer: *Oh, but we have no money. It costs so much to live in Beijing! Are you from Beijing originally?*

Seller: *Actually, I'm from Tianjin. Do you know this city?*

Buyer: *Yes, I went there last month. It is a lovely city. Which do you like better, Beijing or Tianjin?*

Seller: *Certainly I like them both. But maybe Tianjin is a little better, because it's my hometown.*

(The discussion continues for a few minutes...)

Buyer: *Well, you know, I've just noticed this chair has a scratch on the back. That's not good. My husband will think I got taken advantage of if I spend too much. How about 430 kuai for just this one?*

Seller: *Of course there's a scratch! It's an old chair. You won't see it when you put the chair next to a wall. And anyway, I would lose my shop selling at prices like that! How about 550 kuai?*

Buyer: *But that's more than you just quoted! You said 530 kuai.*

Seller: *That's the price if you buy two chairs. Special price. For just one chair, 550 kuai.*

Buyer: *Too much for me. It's more than we planned to spend. Maybe I will discuss it with my husband tonight and see if he will agree to pay more. Thank you!* (Starts to walk away from the booth; there is a pause)

Seller: *Wait, wait, come back. 485 kuai, what do you think? It's an excellent price, right?*

Buyer: (Thinks for a moment) *480 kuai. Please?*

Seller: *OK, OK, 480 kuai. I'll lose money, but you'll be very happy. Do you want a vase, too? I have a nice one over here...*

167

If you had the patience to read the entire dialogue, then you might be one of those expats living in Beijing who shops with a kind of fervor, heartily savoring each *fen* won in the bargaining process; for them, shopping is something more akin to a hobby. But if you skipped more than half of the dialogue, then for you shopping could turn out to be one of the less pleasurable aspects of life in this city.

Even after you have established a relationship with a vendor, you still must bargain. Each sale comes with a certain amount of back-and-forth about price. But the amount of time spent on the process is often reduced, and there are other benefits to being a regular customer—a shopkeeper might know that you collect antique thimbles, for example, and when a particularly nice one comes along will set it aside until your next visit.

MEASUREMENT SYSTEMS

A quick word is in order about how goods and produce are measured in Beijing. While most businesses use the metric system, many smaller ones including market vendors and restaurants go by traditional Chinese measuring units. The most common are:

for length:
- *chi*—a Chinese "foot," or about 0.33m. (10 *chi* = 1 *zhang*)
- *cun*—a Chinese "inch," or about 30cm. (10 *cun* = 1 *chi*)

for weight:
- *jin*—approximately 0.5kg
- *liang*—a tael, or about 0.05kg. (10 *liang* = 1 *jin*)

The measurements listed for weight are frequently used in restaurants for determining the price of whole fish or dumplings. Other Chinese measurements that are less often encountered these

168

days are *zhang* (approximately 3.33m), *dan* (approximately 50kg), and *mu* (a Chinese acre, or just over 0.06 hectares).

❀ ❀ ❀

As you prepare for your shopping jaunts around Beijing, know that over the years, two things have remained constant. One is that if you see something you want, you should buy it—now. Do not wait and mull it over. Whatever you want to purchase will probably not be there when you return. The other is that in Beijing if you work really hard, you can find a great bargain and great quality in the same package. But with most purchases, realize that you are likely to either get a bargain or quality, but not both.

Think of it this way. Whenever you think you've gotten a great deal and instead realize that you've been taken advantage of in a bargaining session, the money that you paid is really your "tuition" for learning how to do things in China.

CHAPTER ELEVEN

MOVING TO BEIJING WITH CHILDREN

TRIGG.

For some parents, the notion of moving to Beijing with their children is fraught with anxiety. They wonder, "Putting ourselves through the turmoil of moving to a new culture is one thing. Are we terrible parents for dragging our children through it as well?" Other parents view the move as a potentially tremendous experience for their children, one that will expose them to the diversity of world cultures. Perhaps both of these perspectives contain some truths.

Generally speaking, the younger your children are, the easier it is for them to adjust to life in Beijing. Most of all, they will take their cue from the adults in the family. Your reactions to the process of adjusting to and appreciating a new life in Beijing will have a direct impact on the adjustment of your children. There are other specific issues, though, that regularly surface in discussions with expat parents.

Chinese families enjoy a winter afternoon in Tiananmen Square.

A "TOUCHING" ISSUE

Chinese people find children quite precious, and most believe that children are basically good until they are taught by society and circumstance to be otherwise. Many Chinese people truly enjoy the presence of children and with well-meaning affection will reach out to touch even the children of strangers. Usually this "touching" involves holding the hands of the children or patting the children on the legs, arms, or cheeks.

Often, the most vigorous attention is showered on non-Asian children, who are often perceived to be exquisite—and the most exquisite ones are blond. A trip to the Forbidden City could take all day if you go there with blond children, because Chinese people will stop you frequently to touch and talk with the children, and might ask to have pictures taken with them.

171

A telling example involves a Western couple and their two children who moved to Beijing. At first they lived in a hotel room while awaiting their household items that were shipped by sea freight. For the first two days, the family ate all meals in the coffee shop of the hotel. While the husband worked, the wife and children took occasional walks; the third day, everyone ventured to the south side of the city to see the Temple of Heaven. That evening, they were notified that their sea shipment had arrived and that they could move to their new home the next day. In particular, the wife was very pleased at how easy life in Beijing seemed to be so far.

The next morning, after moving from the hotel to their new villa, the wife realized that she needed to produce an evening meal for her family. Remembering that there was a grocery store in the basement of the department store near her husband's office, she and the kids headed downtown to do some shopping and to have some lunch.

They entered the store and got a shopping cart, but before they could make any headway down the first aisle, two female Chinese workers appeared. They began talking to the younger child (a blond boy), patting him on the cheeks and arms. Frightened, he grabbed his mother's leg and attempted to hide from the strangers. The older child (a dark-haired girl) had a relatively outgoing personality but because the strangers didn't seem quite as interested in her, she was very disappointed. The boy began to cry, and all the mother wanted to do was grab her children, run from the store, and get on the next plane out of China.

When they finally joined the father for lunch, the mother broke down and cried. She said she felt powerless to help her children out of an uncomfortable predicament. Not only that, but she had left the store without yet purchasing the groceries she needed. It was a very unpleasant way to begin the family's new adventure in Beijing.

This habit of showering attention on children is quite typical in many parts of China, and Chinese people truly do not mean to bring any harm to the children or anxiety to the parents. Unfortunately, the attention is nearly impossible to avoid.

Parents who don't mind their children being in the limelight usually behave the way newly arrived families in the Forbidden City often behave, stopping frequently to allow Chinese people to touch their children and have their pictures taken together. Parents who do not appreciate the attention toward their children can become angry, snatching their children away from strangers as quickly as possible. Others succumb to feeling helpless, the way the mother did after the grocery store incident. In the end, most parents cope by allowing some attention to be paid to their children, and then, with a smile, instructing the children, "Say bye-bye!" and moving on before the picture-taking has a chance to start.

A positive aspect of this attention paid to children is that in restaurants, for example, the wait staff might take fussing children away from the table for a few moments so that the parents can eat in peace. As there are already so many people staffing most enterprises in China, this doesn't really hinder the commercial operations of the restaurants at all.

Some parents say that the attention their children get paid in China makes them a bit spoiled, and that the children then begin to expect this kind of attention from strangers even when they are on leave in their home countries. But given the extent to which children have become even more precious due to China's one-child policy, the excessive attention paid to children there is certainly understandable.

HYGIENE AND HEALTH

We've already mentioned that squeamishness—or one's tolerance for germs and dirt—can be an issue for expats moving to China.

This could be included in the list of issues that pertain to children. In the chapter on *Staying Healthy*, it was mentioned that there is a lot of dust in Beijing. A common complaint of expat parents is that as soon as they get their children clean, they're dirty again. They send the children outdoors to play, and in just five minutes, they're filthy.

If your children play with or near local children, bathroom habits might also be an issue. Rather than using diapers, most Chinese parents, and especially those who are of modest means, dress their small children in pants that are slit from the crotch to the lower back. In order to relieve themselves, the kids just squat and "go." Sometimes the parents hold the children by the thighs so that they are in a sitting position while they do their business. And many local parents are not too concerned about where the child "goes." It is entirely possible to witness a child squatting and "going" in the middle of Tiananmen Square!

Both the issues of dirt and where children go to the bathroom can give parents nightmares about allowing toddlers to run around freely or sit on the ground. Most prevent the nightmares by monitoring their children more closely, like Chinese parents do, or by wheeling them in a stroller as often as possible.

For those parents who hire an *ayi* to help with childcare, a health issue that must be considered is the administration of medicine. Whenever the *ayi* must give some kind of medicine to children, be sure to have the instructions written in Chinese. Also, an issue that should be discussed first with your pediatrician and then with the *ayi* is whether or not you want her to give the children Chinese medicine. Most traditional Chinese medicine is herbal, but it is still medicine. Luckily, most pediatricians working in Beijing should be experienced in issues such as coordinating with an *ayi* to give children medicine, and should have some good advice for you. Be sure to discuss this with your new pediatrician in Beijing well before problems arise.

174

A Chinese toddler, with the convenient split in the seat of the pants.

ADJUSTMENT ISSUES

When it comes to moving to Beijing with kids, there are several adjustment issues that have an impact on the emotional well being of the whole family. These issues vary from family to family, and often depend on the ages of the children at the time of their arrival in China.

An issue for families with infants is maintaining an adequate supply of baby care items. While adults can usually surprise themselves by finding creative ways to go without items that they thought were essential to their very existence, they often do not hold their children to the same standard. They want the best for their offspring. Thus, it is not unheard of for parents living in Beijing to hop onto planes and make one-day shopping excursions to Hong Kong for some "necessity." These parents would never splurge on this type of trip for themselves, but for their children, it's different.

As an example, if you have small children, you have probably already heard and read that it is possible to purchase disposable diapers in Beijing. What no one mentioned, perhaps, is that consistency has never been the strong point of merchants there. Bureaucracy, shipping delays, and other infrastructure snags mean that demand often greatly precedes supply. It is not guaranteed that any store in Beijing will have the type of disposable diaper you need when you need it. Thus, parents in Beijing usually go by three rules: (1) keep a good buffer of stock on hand, (2) supplement the stock while on trips out of the country, and (3) always know what substitutes are available locally in case of desperation.

Related to toddler and baby care items is the subject of toys, and particularly ones that are safe for small children. Many toys and other items for infants and toddlers (such as strollers or prams) that are available in China do not meet the same standards of safety as in some other countries. You can take all the precautions you want within your own home, but Chinese people indulging your children might give them toys that you feel are dangerous. What should you do, for example, if in your presence someone gives your baby something small enough to choke on? Just say a gracious "thank you" and hold the item for your child until you can move away from the person who offered it and surreptitiously dispose of it.

It is common for expats to develop quirks about favorite foods (known as "comfort foods") and other items from their home countries. These items are always things that cannot be found in the host country and may or may not have actually been part of the expats' lives in their home countries. The result is a tendency called "hoarding." On trips home, expats stock up on this comfort food and then ration its use when they return to the host country. Due to the sometimes spotty availability of certain consumer goods in Beijing, hoarding can be exaggerated among expats there. For expats with children old enough to verbalize preferences, it can be taken to an extreme. One mother all but came to believe that her children could not live without individually-wrapped slices of cheese. She would stock it in the freezer, carefully doling it out to the children one slice at a time. At one point, she caught her husband unwrapping a slice for himself. She screamed at him, "Don't you dare eat that! It's for the children!"

Some parents who have hired one or more *ayis* to assist with domestic chores struggle with the behavior of their children. Some children stop taking responsibility for themselves at home, leaving their bedrooms messy, believing that it is the *ayi's* job to pick up after them. Others become bossy, perhaps ordering the *ayis* to pick up their toys or clean their bedrooms.

The parents of older children, such as teenagers, generally find that their children enjoy life in Beijing. Taxis are cheap and plentiful, offering teen students an easy way to take advantage of all the stimulating activities that the city has to offer. However, some teenagers take advantage of the absence of a legal drinking age in China, and there is talk of "club drugs" making their way onto the streets of Beijing. It is wise to set some boundaries for older children.

When experiencing culture shock, teenagers exhibit some of the same tendencies as adults. Most often, the symptoms are either overeating or isolation. Do not be too concerned if your teenager locks him- or herself in the bedroom for several days after a few months in your new home. Allow your teenager some "space" and time to adjust. Non-verbal support can be helpful. Deliver meals to your isolationist in the bedroom. Make sure there is plenty of low-calorie, nutritious food around for the overeater. If the behavior continues for more than 10 days or so, seek professional assistance.

SCHOOLS

Parents moving to Beijing with children should begin researching schools as early as possible. The *Resource Guide* provides some leads. In some cases, the school you choose for your children might determine the neighborhood in which you will want to live. Another consideration might be how long you will be staying in Beijing, as some schools only provide education up to certain grade levels.

The native language of the parents and the language of instruction in the schools children will attend after they leave Beijing can also be deciding factors in choosing schools. Most international schools use a foreign language such as English as the language of primary instruction, offering occasional specialized classes in Chinese. Some parents choose to enroll their children in Chinese schools for the intense exposure to Mandarin and written Chinese, although the number of Chinese schools that will accept foreign students is still limited.

A difficult issue concerning schools in Beijing involves the paucity of resources for children of school age who have learning disabilities or other special needs. Adequate professional assistance for these children might not be available in Beijing, so be sure to talk with school officials to see what resources exist before making the decision to move there.

Depending on the level and manner of teaching at previous schools attended, some children will find certain subjects taught in the international schools too easy. Other children will find that these schools are rigorous and will require a period of adjustment. Extra-curricular activities might be different from those the newcomers expected. In addition to athletic and musical activities, most of the international schools focus a certain amount of attention on teaching children about the local environment, offering field trips to sites of interest around Beijing and to other parts of China.

❈ ❈ ❈

Life in Beijing can expose children to the marvels of the global community. Through their experiences in the international schools, they are likely to make friends from many parts of the world. Only occasionally do they turn into "expat brats"—the result of being waited on by an *ayi* and doted on by parents who feel guilty for hauling them off to China.

Most of all, as mentioned earlier, children get their cues from their parents as to how to interact with the local environment. The way you handle your experiences in Beijing will to a great extent determine how well your children adapt.

— Chapter Twelve —

LEISURE

Probably the most popular forms of recreation in Beijing, among outsiders and local people alike, are eating and shopping. Expat families head to parks on the weekends for picnics or venture off to explore new neighborhoods. Some expats enjoy getting clothes made at local tailor shops, while others are tired from a hectic week and simply want to collapse onto the sofa and watch a movie. There are plenty of other ways to be entertained and spend leisure time in Beijing, with new ones surfacing almost daily.

INSIDER'S LIST

Once you have settled into your new home in Beijing, you will probably want to begin exploring all that the city has to offer.

Most people know about sites such as the Forbidden City and the Great Wall, which are visited by most tourists to Beijing and are well described in many tourist guides. Generally speaking, it is best to visit these highly popular tourist sites between November and March when there are substantially fewer foreign visitors. The tourist season is considered to run from April 1 through October 31 each year.

Especially during tourist season when popular sites are crowded, many expats enjoy exploring locations that are off the well-beaten tourist path. The ones listed here are favorites among expats as places to take short-term visitors, or to explore on weekends with other residents of Beijing. Visiting them is a way to take advantage of all that your new home has to offer, as they provide truly unique Beijing experiences. The Chinese names for these sites are listed in the *Glossary*.

Ancient Temples

Two of the oldest temples in Beijing are outside the city, resting in peace and tranquility in the Mentougou District. The larger one, Tanzhe Temple (*tan* means pool; *zhe* is a type of tree similar to the mulberry), is said to be the oldest Buddhist temple in Beijing. The other, Jietai Temple (*jietai* is usually translated as "ordination terrace"), is also very old, dating from 622 A.D. It might be possible to visit both of these temples in one long morning if you leave Beijing very early and plan on a late lunch when you return, but it is best to allot an entire leisurely day to see them.

Confucius Temple (Capital Museum) and the Imperial Academy

Tucked away, side by side, in the northeast corner of the Second Ring Road are these two famous sites, more often visited by Chinese tourists than by foreigners. These sites have not been as thoroughly renovated as some other locations in the city, although

181

more work has been done on the temple than on the academy. At the Confucius Temple, don't overlook the tablets inscribed with the *Thirteen Classics* housed along the left side of the temple, or the museum of Beijing history along the right. The Imperial Academy is not to be missed if only for its serene setting; it was the place where scholars prepared for the civil service examinations and where the emperor occasionally gave lectures on the classics. After you have seen these two sites, wander around in the *hutong* to the west for some flavor of old Beijing, or visit the tranquil teahouse across the street.

To get to these sites by taxi, tell the driver that you want to go to the Imperial Academy (point to the Chinese characters in this book or in another guidebook—many Beijingers do not know where the Confucius Temple is located, and it is unlikely that your driver will recognize the name "Imperial Academy" in English). To get to these temples on foot, first go to the main entrance of the Lama Temple. (Get off at the Yonghegong stop if taking the

A series of archways leads to the Temple of Heaven.

subway and walk south.) Then, walk north from the Lama Temple entrance and take the first road to the left under the ornate archway. The Confucius Temple and the Imperial Academy are both on the north side of the street.

"Cosmological Altars"

The four "cosmological altars" located in Beijing are the Temple of Heaven (*tiantan*), the Temple of Earth (*ditan*), the Temple of the Moon (*yuetan*), and the Temple of the Sun (*ritan*). (Most guidebooks and maps in English use the word "temple" for *tan*; however, "altar" would be a more accurate translation.) It will take you a good day and a half, if not two days, to visit all four of them. Although the Temple of Heaven is by far the most well known and impressive of these shrines to cosmological forces, in traditional Chinese thinking it is the balance among them that is most important. They are perceived by Chinese people to be in opposite, complementary pairs. The Temple of Heaven on the south side of the city is paired with the Temple of Earth on the north side. The Temple of the Sun on the east side is the *yang* (light) to the *yin* (dark) of the Temple of the Moon on the west side. The emperor was thought to play an intermediary role in harmonizing these cosmological forces for the common people, and could best do so from the central location of the Forbidden City. At appropriate times of the year, the emperor also performed ritual ceremonies at each of these "altars."

In some of these temples, you will notice that the exterior walls are in a square pattern and that some interior structures are round. This is because Chinese people traditionally thought that heaven was round and earth was square. Nowadays, with the exception of the Temple of Heaven, the "cosmological altars" are better known as quiet parks where local people can chat, relax, fish, or play Chinese chess. The park surrounding the Temple of the Sun is known for its outdoor restaurants that serve great food

183

at reasonable prices — try the one just to the east of the southwest corner of the park. At the Temple of Earth, walk along the east side of the park and you might get to see a leisurely croquet match.

Hutong Tour

With the old *hutong* rapidly disappearing from the Beijing landscape, many people are hoping that at least the neighborhoods visited in the official *hutong* tours will be preserved. Several different tour operators now offer rides in covered pedicabs through the back alleys of Beijing. You can purchase tickets at many of the major hotels and tourism offices in the city. Pick a nice day, as you will spend most of the time outdoors. These tours offer a taste of old Beijing and feature stops at homes along the way and chats with current residents. Bilingual tour guides describe the construction methods used to build courtyard homes

A doorway in Prince Gong's Palace, which is a regular stop on the Hutong Tour.

found along the *hutong* and methods for determining the status of residents during imperial times. This is a colorful way to spend a half day in Beijing.

Panjiayuan Dirt Market
Held on Sunday mornings, this outdoor market in the southeast part of the city is something to behold. Expats gave it the name "dirt market" because about one-quarter of the market is in open air, with goods displayed on sheets of cloth spread over the dirt. The name also refers to the conjecture that some of the goods are not really antiques, but modern wares rubbed with a bit of dirt. There's something for everyone at this market—antique furniture, carpets, paintings, and a wide assortment of trinkets and curios, such as brass locks for Chinese cabinets. Here, it is essential to practice the art of bargaining, and the maxim "buyer beware" has never been more important to follow.

Underground City
During the Mao years, a series of tunnels was created under the city of Beijing. Some say this was to protect the people of Beijing in the event of a nuclear attack, and some say it was to provide government officials and military personnel a secure way of moving around the city. Whatever the case, portions of these tunnels are now open for tours. Go with a group of friends, as a trip through the underground passageways can feel darned spooky. It helps if one of your friends can read Chinese characters, as many of the street signs along the way to the entrance are in Chinese characters only. From Qianmen, head south and bear left into the first small street (Xidamochang Jie). Take several steps to where the street forks; bear to the right. After about 10 minutes' walk, No. 62 is on the right-hand side of the street. You can purchase your ticket here, and a guide will escort you through the tunnels.

White Cloud Temple

Most temples in the city of Beijing are Buddhist, but this one is Taoist. As it is off the beaten path for tourists, it can be a relatively peaceful place to visit. The site of the temple dates back to the Tang Dynasty. Taoist deities are honored here, and you might see temple staff members wearing traditional Chinese-style clothing and hairstyles. Be sure to explore and enter gateways wherever it is permitted, as the temple contains several small courtyards.

A unique feature of the White Cloud Temple is its three-arch gate.

Other short excursions that expats in Beijing enjoy are:

- Visiting Chengde, a former imperial summer resort area in Hebei Province that is about a four-hour train ride from Beijing;

186

- Exploring all of the various sites along the Great Wall, such as Simatai, Badaling, Mutianyu, and Jinshanling—a trip to any one of these will take the better part of a day;
- Visiting the neighboring city of Tianjin, a port city which is about two hours' train ride from Beijing—plan a full day for a trip there, and be sure that you know what time the last train leaves to return to Beijing;
- Camping overnight in Shidu, which is a couple of hours' drive from Beijing—horseback riding is possible there during the day, but the racket from firecracker concessions can be quite jarring;
- Visiting the Western Qing Tombs on the southwest side of the city;
- Picnicking at the Old Summer Palace and at various parks around the city.

MUSEUMS

Located in the large stone building on the eastern side of Tiananmen Square is the National Museum of Chinese History. In addition to the permanent exhibit, there is usually at least one featured exhibit. Exhibits can vary greatly in terms of entrance fees, display lighting, and the quality of care taken with the objects. As for labels and written explanations, most are in Chinese and some are translated into English. Audio tours are sometimes available for the exhibits, but again they can range in terms of quality as well as in the languages offered. North of the National Museum of Chinese History, in the same building, is the Museum of the Chinese Revolution.

For an exhibit on the history of Beijing, visit the Capital Museum, which is housed in the Confucius Temple on the northeast side of the city. Please see the *Insider's List* earlier in this chapter for more information.

187

NIGHT LIFE

There are so many spots for evening recreation in Beijing that it is impossible to list them all. However, there are two primary areas in which foreigners tend to congregate. One is near the Worker's Stadium, and the other is on the east side of the Third Ring Road.

To get to the first one, ask a taxi to take you to the City Hotel just east of the Workers' Stadium. In English, the hotel is sometimes also called the Chains City Hotel (in Mandarin, Chengshi Binguan). From there, walk south. On your left will be Frank's Place, the first joint venture Western restaurant in the city. If you are dying for a hamburger, this is a good place to go. Just a few steps further south will bring you to Berena's, a well-known expat hangout for generous portions of quite delicious Chinese food. The lighting is low, the staff speaks some English, and the menu is in both English and Chinese.

After you've eaten your fill at either Frank's Place or Berena's, walk north to the main road. Turn right and then right again into the first large alleyway. Here you can visit several lively night spots, such as Minder Café or Durty Nellie's for drinks and some live music.

The second general area for nightly relaxation is just outside the Third Ring Road on the east side of Beijing. Try Schiller's 3 at the west gate of Chaoyang Park for dinner, and then head south to the bar area. (Ask for directions at Schiller's 3. Many of the night spots that were formerly located on Sanlitun Bar Street have moved to this new site.) You'll have several places to choose from, such as the Big Easy (on your right as you enter the bar neighborhood), which offers either jazz or blues most evenings.

PERFORMANCE ARTS

A popular event each week in Beijing is the Friday night showing of Chinese movies with subtitles at the Cherry Lane Theater. Originally organized by Sophia Boccio and called "Sophia's

Choice," this weekly event provides expats who do not speak Chinese an opportunity to learn something about Chinese culture through film. Certain films have been independently subtitled by Cherry Lane and thus might never be seen with subtitles elsewhere in the world.

As for foreign films, one can buy DVDs, CDs, and VCDs produced in several languages all over town. Not all of these are legal copies, so keep in mind that if you carry or send them to another country, they may be confiscated there.

Other types of performance art accessible in Beijing are Chinese acrobatics, orchestra performances, the ballet, and — of course! — Peking Opera. Check foreign language newspapers for listings of these performances, or ask Chinese friends and colleagues for their recommendations.

RELIGION

Meetings for people of almost every religious faith can now be found in Beijing. There are Catholic churches, Muslim mosques, and Jewish and Protestant gatherings. Some embassies offer religious services at their diplomatic compounds. People who wish to attend certain services must be able to show foreign passports, while other services are open to everyone.

Many of the Catholic churches in Beijing can be difficult to locate on maps. Probably the most famous one is Beitang, which is located just west of Beihai Park. (*Tang* is short for *jiaotang* meaning "church"; some English-language guidebooks translate it as "cathedral." The *bei* means "north." In Beijing there is also a Nantang or "South Church," a Xitang or "West Church," and a Dongtang or "East Church.") Dongtang is the easiest to find, as it is located smack in the middle of the popular shopping street, Wangfujing. Services in English are few at these churches; most services are offered either in Chinese or in Latin.

189

There are two or three Muslim mosques open for services in the city. Perhaps the best known is the Niujie Mosque in the Xuanwu District. People wearing shorts or skirts are generally not allowed to enter these mosques, and there are separate worship areas for men and women. Non-Muslims are generally not allowed to enter the prayer halls.

Jewish services are offered each week at the Capital Club Athletic Center. An online newsletter provides announcements of activities within the Jewish community in Beijing. (Refer to the *Resource Guide* for more information.)

Two inter-denominational Protestant groups have been meeting regularly for a few years. One of them, the Beijing International Christian Fellowship, meets at the Sino-Japanese Youth Exchange Center just outside the Third Ring Road on the northeast side of the city. Another, some say more conservative, Protestant group called the Church of the Good Shepherd meets in the Capital Club Athletic Center.

If you are interested in joining any of the activities of these religious groups, or in learning about other gatherings, check current listings or ask other expats for an update once you have arrived in Beijing.

BOOKS AND NEWSPAPERS

There are numerous bookstores in the city stocking Chinese-language books, but foreign language books are a bit more difficult to find. Unless they are published in China, books in foreign languages can also be rather expensive. The Foreign Language Bookstore, the most popular store dedicated to selling foreign books is located on Wangfujing—the main shopping street in the heart of town. The Friendship Store in Jianguomenwai also has a large selection of books that expats might want to read, and many hotels offer smaller selections. Overall, most of the hotels are inconsistent in what they stock, so expats develop the habit of popping into the gift shop each time they enter a hotel just to see what's available at the moment.

In terms of other foreign language materials, the *China Daily* newspaper is printed in English and offers mostly domestic news items from a local perspective. Available at hotel gift shops are international editions of many publications such as *Time* magazine, the *International Herald Tribune*, and the *Asian Wall Street Journal*.

❊ ❊ ❊

It should be noted that the organization of activities for expats living in Beijing often depends on enthusiastic, charismatic leaders to keep groups going. With the expat community always in a state of flux, activities can change location or disappear at the drop of a hat. Check with other expats upon your arrival to see which leisure activities are currently popular.

In general, though, the wide variety of activities and resources available for expats living in Beijing these days not only enhances their enjoyment of the city, but brings local culture into more accessible range.

CHAPTER THIRTEEN

WORKING IN BEIJING

Being invited to work in Beijing can be a heady experience. Often, expats feel flattered to be asked to make important contributions to the economic, academic, or technological development of China and its people. Expat positions can be highly visible both in the sending organization and within the Beijing work environment.

Then come the realities of work. The way expats accomplished things before might not be the best way to accomplish them in China. Unmet expectations can lead to disappointment and sometimes even failure. Learning as much as they can about the business environment can help expats decide whether or not to take an assignment in China and prepare them to manage the challenges that await.

MAKING THE DECISION

Perhaps your employer is proposing that you open an office for the company in Beijing. Perhaps you are of Chinese heritage and want your children to learn Mandarin and be immersed in Chinese culture. Perhaps your expertise is required to further develop your company's position in the China market. Perhaps you are a native speaker of a foreign language that is popular in China, such as Russian or English, and crave the adventure of living in another culture, deciding to put your skills to work as a language teacher. Whatever the case, the decision to work in Beijing should not be made lightly.

By now you know some of the personal issues that should be considered when weighing your decision. Among them are the depth of your interest in Chinese culture and language, the state of your health, the tolerance you have concerning cleanliness, and whether or not you have children.

One of the worst reasons to decide to accept an assignment in Beijing is "for the money." While many employers still classify China locations as "hardship posts," thus offering increased compensation and benefits to foreign employees who agree to live there, it is rare for foreigners to be able to salt away any real savings. The reasons for this are several. Some foreigners, especially when they are experiencing culture shock, try desperately to simulate their lives in their home countries. Instead of developing a taste for a typical Chinese breakfast of soy milk and *youtiao* (stick donuts; literally, "oily stick"), they want a breakfast cereal like the one they ate at home even though it costs US$8 per box. When they run out of dental floss, they are amazed

193

that it costs US$10 to replace. After a few days of Chinese lunches, they want a good meal from their home country, which always costs at least 25% more than local fare, and in many places costs triple. During vacations, they certainly don't stay in Beijing. Some travel around China or visit other locations in Asia, but most return home and spend lavishly for the duration of the trip. Frankly, few foreigners in Beijing save much money during their stays.

For some people, a serious issue that is present in all of China, but is most acute in Beijing, is coping with a relatively strict socialist regime. Expats who cannot behave within the bounds of what is acceptable to the government of China, or who cannot refrain from speaking poorly about central government edicts (such as the one-child policy), should stay away from Beijing. While occasional venting among expats is to be expected, indiscriminate complaints or criticisms of the government are invitations for authorities to make life difficult.

If at all possible, one step in making the decision to live and work in China should be to take a short trip to the capital. Talk with as many people as you can, especially people who are in a similar professional position to the one you would accept. Visit expats in their homes and ask them what are their favorite aspects of living in Beijing as well as their biggest complaints. Resist the temptation to visit every famous tourist site, and instead venture out of your hotel for walks. Visit some of the places you and your family are likely to frequent, such as shops, schools, and hospitals. It will give you a feeling for local life, as well as for the lifestyle you and your family might experience in Beijing.

In spite of the challenges, many expats find working in Beijing stimulating and rewarding. The yet untapped potential of China and the people who live there seems exciting and, at times, limitless. Above all, intrinsic curiosity and interest in the culture and history of China's people on the part of an expat can make working in Beijing a truly satisfying and enriching experience.

STARTING OUT

Once you have arrived in Beijing, no matter what your work will entail, it is likely that your first few weeks will be filled with introductory meetings. Depending on your position in the organization, you might be meeting new colleagues, bosses, customers, subordinates, vendors, or students. The guidelines for making a good impression offered earlier in this book will certainly apply to your initial encounters with everyone. In the work setting, an additional component of the impression you make on others involves establishing your credibility. The way this is done in China may be different from how it is done in your culture.

In general, demonstrating some modesty about your professional background creates a better impression than does talking openly about it. Most likely everyone already knows a fair amount about you, as it is common practice to circulate information on the background of newcomers before their arrival in Beijing. The person introducing you to others during the first couple of weeks will probably add more information about your credentials and accomplishments. It is important during this introduction stage for you to focus more attention on learning about others than on giving them information about yourself. For example, find out which part of China people are originally from—never assume they are all Beijingers. Offer modest responses to any compliments that come your way. Tell people your positive impressions of Beijing and its citizens. If you will be in a managerial position, it will make a good impression on local workers if you know something about their achievements and efforts. Better yet, acknowledge their previous accomplishments, even though you might be planning to change some systems and procedures that were developed before your arrival. In a corporate setting, it is important to stress how your work with people in the Beijing office will benefit China and its people rather than stressing how the stockholders in your employer's home country will benefit.

Overall, folks in Beijing tend to be more formal, and perhaps more stoic, than people in other parts of China. During your first meetings with Beijingers, please don't fidget! Neither should you lean forward when seated, as this can make you appear anxious or aggressive. Instead, maintain an upright, formal posture with both feet on the floor in order to give others the impression that you are a trustworthy person worth getting to know. As time goes by, follow the lead of your Chinese counterparts as to when and how to relax your posture and demeanor.

EXCHANGING BUSINESS CARDS

In China, one aspect of being a credible professional is having business cards and being able to exchange them with others in culturally appropriate ways. The first step is to have business cards prepared with Chinese on one side and English (or your native language) on the other side. Again, be sure to ask an educated Chinese person to help you with this and with choosing a Chinese name. At first, if you do not have cards with Chinese on them, it is acceptable to give out cards in just your native language until your bilingual cards are ready. Something that is considered rather inappropriate is to hand out cards that are printed in your native language on one side and in Japanese on the other. Instead, make photocopies of the side of the card printed in your native language until your cards with Chinese on them are ready. Of course, if you are Japanese and have cards with only Japanese on them, it is fine to give those out.

When exchanging business cards, people who are considered guests or visitors should present their cards to others first. Within your organization, those who are equal or below you in rank will probably present their cards to you first, as they are likely to perceive you as a "foreign expert." The sequence in which cards are given out is usually in descending order of seniority; in other words, people present their cards to the most senior people first.

(If there is a large group of people, then lower-ranking people will often exchange cards while the senior people do the same. Then members of each group exchange cards with members of the other group.) In Beijing you are likely to meet many government officials; the highest-ranking ones usually do not participate in the exchange of business cards, with the assumption being that everyone already knows who they are.

As you meet each person, shake hands while nodding slightly and then present your card with both hands. Be sure to turn your card so that the writing is legible to your counterparts as they receive it. When you receive their cards, accept them with both hands as well. Treat the cards respectfully, as they represent the individuals whose names they bear. Read the cards, and confirm family names and titles. Ask for assistance with the pronunciation of people's names. Do your best to refer to your counterparts or colleagues by their family names plus their titles (for example, Manager Li or Director Chen), or Miss, Mr or Madame plus the family name as appropriate. (Refer to the chapter on *People and Culture* for additional guidance on this topic.) It is a good idea to make some small talk to get acquainted. Then move on to accept the business card of the next person. If everyone will be sitting down for a meeting after the exchange of cards, people usually arrange on the table in front of them the business cards that they have just received.

ATTENDING BANQUETS

The ability to get things done in Chinese culture hinges on having good relationships, or *guanxi*, with people who can help—and there's no better way to build *guanxi* with others than to have banquets. Chinese people consider sharing meals an essential component of getting acquainted and building relationships; in fact, the comment, "We've shared many meals together" means, "We have a very close relationship." Once you have built a strong relationship, any endeavor is likely to proceed more smoothly.

197

The term "banquet" can be used in several different ways. Many expats and foreign visitors use the English word to mean a dinner attended by people one knows from one's work, such as colleagues, vendors, and customers. Some expats use it to describe any Chinese meal attended by more than four people, at least one of whom is Chinese. In the case of a noontime meal, English-speakers mostly refer to "lunch banquets." By itself, however, "banquet" generally means an evening meal. In contrast to this very broad use of the word "banquet" in English, Chinese people use *yanhui* (the customary translation of "banquet" primarily to refer to very formal meals. In this book, we use the term to mean dinners or lunches that are pre-arranged, include at least six people, and are at least moderately formal.

Among Chinese people, there are certain occasions on which banquets are customary and expected. Banquets are held in the initial stages of developing a professional relationship as a way of showing respect and hospitality, as well as showing that one values the prospective relationship. Banquets are also held to celebrate important milestones, such as a contract signing or the opening of a new facility. Occasionally, if certain discussions or work in general are not proceeding smoothly, banquets can also provide a forum for "informal" conversations through which difficult issues can be identified and resolved.

While you are living in Beijing, there are likely to be plenty of occasions on which you will be the honored guest at a Chinese banquet. It is therefore essential to learn how to be a good guest. In essence, the role of the guest is to show respect, appreciation, and gratitude to the host. Show respect by allowing your hosts to arrive at the restaurant first so that they can greet you when you arrive, but do not arrive so late that you keep your hosts waiting long. Show appreciation by praising the quality and quantity of food. Show gratitude by offering a return toast if the host has made a toast in your honor. (For additional guidelines, see the chapter on *The Chinese Dining Experience*.)

When offering toasts at formal banquets, it is wise to convey a positive tone and not be too specific about the work at hand — rather than talking about profitability, speak of mutual benefit; instead of saying that you look forward to getting down to work, refer to a future of friendly cooperation and success.

For toasts and to accompany the meal, diners at formal Chinese banquets are generally offered a choice of beverages such as beer, soft drinks, wine, and perhaps hard liquor. (Maotai is the most famous brand of hard liquor in China. Made from sorghum, it is quite potent, with about a 60% alcohol content.) Although the word for "cheers" is *ganbei*, or literally, "dry glass," it is usually not necessary to actually empty your glass when each toast is made. Just taking a sip is fine if you don't want to drink too much. However, it is the responsibility of members of the host party to energetically encourage guests to drink their fill; thus, your neighbors at the table are likely to "cheer" you on to drink more. Each time they do, just take another small sip. At some large banquets, the most senior person in each party goes to each table to make a toast, accompanied by a more junior member. In these cases, the senior person takes only a sip after each toast, while the junior person empties his or her glass to encourage guests to do the same.

If you don't drink for religious or other reasons, it is best to simply put the glass to your lips for each toast, but not drink. It is also acceptable to tell Chinese people that you *can't* drink (although to Chinese banquet participants, it might seem rather unsportsmanlike). Depending on your hosts' exposure to other cultures, stating that one does not drink for religious reasons, for example, might not be readily understood. Non-drinkers should at least use a soft drink to participate in each toast.

A unique feature of Chinese banquets is the manner in which food is served. When dishes are brought to the table, they are placed on a circular, revolving platform ("lazy Susan") in the middle of the table. This platform makes it easy for large numbers of people to share the banquet dishes. As each person takes food from one of the serving plates, it is considered polite to then spin the platform slightly to the left for the next person to be served.

An important consideration at formal banquets is whether or not to discuss work, and how to approach work topics on such occasions. Most Chinese people consider banquets to be primarily social events, so extensive discussions of work-related topics may be considered gauche and inappropriate. However, brief exchanges of very general or "casual" remarks or questions are not unusual. In fact, these could be hints concerning critical issues about which your local counterparts have concerns. Naturally, you can use these same techniques yourself. Given the potential importance of such exchanges, it is critical either to have competent interpreters present, or a Chinese person who can assist you in understanding the remarks of others and in composing your own. In other words, in spite of the festive spirit of banquets, always keep your wits about you. Otherwise, you might innocently agree to something that you will truly regret later!

Sometimes the festive spirit of a banquet will continue with a visit to a *karaoke* club, where guests and hosts can sing away the evening. However, this is not as common in Beijing as in some other places in East Asia. It is somewhat rare to make a stop at a bar or nightclub after a banquet.

HOSTING BANQUETS

When living in Beijing for an extended period of time, there are likely to be occasions when you will host banquets—if only to return the honor of having been invited to banquets by others. Don't be shy about initiating invitations to banquets. Whether you wish to smooth relations with officials, build ties among subordinates, elevate the mood of discussions with Chinese counterparts, or simply return a favor, it's time to host a banquet.

200

In business, perhaps even more so than in social situations, it's important to keep the scales balanced. If you are involved in negotiations, for example, Chinese participants in the proceedings might try to extract more concessions than normal from you, if they feel their side is "owed" something.

If you don't know of a suitable restaurant at which to hold your banquet, it is a good idea to ask a Chinese person whom you know well to help you choose one. A person you know is likely to suggest a reputable place for an honest price. A person you don't know well might steer you toward a restaurant owned by a friend, whether or not that restaurant is appropriate for your needs. The person might even suggest that the restaurant owner charge you 15% more than normal, because it is widely assumed that foreigners are rich.

Many expats prefer to host banquets in upscale Chinese restaurants in good hotels such as the China World or Jing Guang. The price of the meal will be higher than what could be negotiated at some local restaurants, but the benefit is that many staff members speak English and can professionally assist you in making arrangements. Additionally, you give your guests face by holding the banquet at such a high-status venue. Yet another possibility is to host a banquet at a restaurant where you've attended a banquet in the past.

Inviting your Chinese counterparts to an informal meal at a Western restaurant is acceptable if the meal is served buffet-style. This allows your guests to select food by viewing the actual dishes rather than by trying to decipher a menu. This minimizes discomfort for Chinese guests who may have had relatively little exposure to Western food. When it comes right down to it, though, most Chinese people really prefer to eat Chinese food.

After you've chosen the restaurant, the next step in hosting a Chinese banquet is selecting the food. This should be done at least one day in advance for formal dinners. Again, ask a Chinese person you know well and who knows something about your relationship with the guests to assist you in choosing the proper menu items. If you don't, this person might suggest only the most expensive items on the menu. In some cases, you can enlist the assistance of the restaurant staff during a quiet time of the day; going to the restaurant in person to discuss the menu and other arrangements is best.

While people are likely to fight for the bill at informal meals, this is usually not the case with banquets. It is acceptable to pay the bill at the table, but it is better to have one of your colleagues make payment away from the table, or to arrange with the restaurant for you to pay the bill after the guests have left. Whoever pays the bill should review the bill item by item, comparing it to the original agreement with the restaurant and asking the restaurant to explain any charges that differ from those agreed upon in previous discussions.

When you host a banquet and especially if you decide to schedule an after-banquet activity, it is important to arrange transportation home for certain guests, especially customers and subordinates. People who rode their bicycles to work might prefer to be taken back to their work units to retrieve them, but those who took buses might have missed the last one home. In this case, as the host, you should assist in hailing one or more taxis and should pay for the taxi fares. Ask a Chinese colleague for guidance on appropriately arranging transportation home for your guests.

DEALING WITH BUREAUCRACY

As the capital of the country, Beijing is the locus of national government ministries and other bureaucratic agencies. Many foreign enterprises have chosen to locate their China headquarters in the capital in order for their management personnel to have regular contact and build *guanxi* with government officials. Professors and scholars living in Beijing must deal with government officials as well, as universities are public institutions. Essentially, regular dealings with government officials are an inescapable part of working in Beijing.

At one time, government agencies were intimately involved in most aspects of business in China. A foreign company's customers, vendors, and workers were all employees of government institutions. Nowadays, bureaucracies are less involved in day-to-day issues, and some expats believe that government officials are permitted to be more flexible than in the past. But other expats suggest that it was easier to deal with government agencies when the behavior of officials was more regimented, as responsibilities among officials and agencies overlapped less. Currently, many government officials and agencies compete for jurisdiction over certain business issues, so there can be several different ways of getting the same thing done. It is rarely clear which might be the best path.

For outsiders who come to work in Beijing, success requires keeping in close touch with key officials whose decisions might have an impact on work efforts, and carefully monitoring shifts in

government policies. Learning how to effectively persuade and cajole Beijing bureaucrats is another critical skill. To expats whose skills in these areas are not well developed, the bureaucracy can seem like a huge, impersonal, unreasonable impediment to getting work done. In some cases, frustration with bureaucracy has pushed expats "over the edge" and they have departed from Beijing without completing the full terms of their assignments.

A situation that commonly frustrates expats is that officials seem unwilling to explain procedures, rules, internal workings, and bureaucratic requirements. When you ask how to get a project approved, officials might say, "Fill this out," providing no further elucidation or instruction. After you have submitted the documents and you check back to see how long it will be before your project is approved, they might say, "Come back in person next week." (This could go on for several weeks.) When they reject your documents and you ask why, they might say, "You did not include XYZ form." The expat wonders why no one mentioned "XYZ form" to begin with.

Here is a scenario that illustrates the process of talking with a government official about an ongoing project. Let's say that you have received a telephone call from a customer, stating that the customer cannot retrieve from Customs a shipment being sent from your home office. Upon visiting the Customs office, the following exchange takes place:

You: *Our customers had some trouble clearing their shipment under Contract No. 1234. Can you tell us what the problem is?*

Officer: *The shipping documents do not match the goods.*

You: *Could you tell me which items do not match?*

Officer: *Your company should be more careful with your shipments.*

You: *We try to do our best for our customers. Could you give me some more specific information about this problem?*

Officer: *Foreign companies are always doing sloppy work and then trying to blame the problems on us. They take advantage of our local customers.*

You: *We are certainly not trying to take advantage of our customers. If you could tell me more about this problem, I am sure that we can resolve it easily.*

Officer: *Perhaps you should contact your home office and tell them to correct their mistakes. They should be more careful in the future.*

Several things could be happening in this example. The Customs official could feel backed into a corner. This often occurs when expats try to discuss urgent matters with the first officials they encounter. An official who is not personally familiar with a given case is unlikely to be able to discuss it in any detail. You might have been better off starting the discussion by asking, "Could I talk with someone concerning the shipment for Contract No. 1234?" It is also not the job of officials to explain decisions or rules. Asking what is wrong with documents or with your actions puts officials in an awkward position. Telling you what you did wrong makes you lose face. A better approach is to ask the official, "What is the best solution to this situation?" In other words, solicit the advice and assistance of officials rather than demanding explanations.

It is rare for bureaucrats in Beijing to feel any need to explain the inner workings of their operations and the decisions they make. In this case, perhaps the customers rushed to get their goods before Customs officials had completed their work. The officials are unlikely to mention that this is the real reason for the delay.

Most likely, the problem in this scenario was caused by inconsistencies between the shipping documents and the original contract. For example, perhaps a substitution was made for an item that was discontinued or not in stock. Changes such as this can cause headaches and skepticism among bureaucrats in Beijing. From their perspective, questions arise. Is this company trying to take advantage of our people? Is the customer trying to cheat on the duties they are supposed to pay? Unless and until all issues are satisfactorily explained, delays will occur.

So what can expats do to work more effectively with bureaucracy? Here are some savvy ways to cope:

- Allow local staff members to handle matters with officials rather than always trying to handle them yourself. The way bureaucracies operate is often strongly influenced by the general culture of the society in which they function, and local people will probably know best how to handle matters within their own culture.
- When you must handle issues yourself, ask to speak with an appropriate official or individual who has access to information about your specific situation. Wait until this person can talk with you, rather than launching into discussions with anyone who will listen.
- Be conscious of face — both yours and that of officials. Avoid questions and responses that might cause anyone to lose face.
- When talking with officials, focus on solutions rather than searching for explanations.
- Check documentation to ensure there are no errors, omissions, changes, or inconsistencies. Surprises often cause bureaucratic delays.
- Build and use your *guanxi* wisely. An underlying principle of life in China is a preference for *renzhi* (rule of person) as opposed to *fazhi* (rule of law). Develop relationships with officials at multiple levels who can help you accomplish things in appropriate ways.

- Understand that "the back door is sometimes the front door," as expats often say. Instead of beating yourself up trying to accomplish something one way, try a different method. The results might surprise you.
- Recognize that dealing with bureaucracy is a fact of life in Beijing. Acceptance can go a long way toward making your interaction with bureaucrats seem more manageable.

For foreigners, it is also important to realize that relations between your country and China can sometimes have an impact on your dealings with bureaucrats. In times of tension, it can be harder to work together. If relations with your country are a current national priority, however, things might go quite smoothly.

LOCAL EMPLOYEES

Expats who go to work in Beijing will probably find themselves working not just with Beijingers, but with a diverse group of people from all over China. Some of the best universities in China, notably Beijing University and Qinghua University, are located in Beijing. As national universities, they draw students from all over the country. Graduates of these universities have long been eagerly sought as employees by both Chinese and foreign organizations as sources of skills and talent.

This diversity among Beijing workers contributes to a rich pool of talent. However, informal ties and networks based on similarities in dialects and regional cultures can sometimes pose challenges to communication, cooperation, and teamwork among Chinese staff members. Awareness of and an ability to manage this issue is an important factor in the success of expats working in Beijing.

Another important consideration to keep in mind is that local nationals, like people everywhere, want to be treated with dignity and respect. Mutual respect can be challenging to maintain when disparities in education, professional skills, and work experience are apparent. The expectations of expats concerning the job performance of local employees are often inordinately high, given the resources available to local workers and the relatively brief amount of time that China has been open to the outside world.

The expectations of local employees concerning the job performance of expats can also be extremely high. Most expats who are working in Beijing on full expat packages are paid several times more than local employees. With housing and other allowances added to salary, expat packages can be worth a hundred times more than the package of a typical Chinese worker. Local employees might expect the performance of expats to be commensurate with these extraordinary compensation packages. When problems occur and expats do not know how to resolve them appropriately, local people wonder if the expats are worth the drain on their organization's financial resources.

For the most part, local workers also have high expectations for expats of Chinese heritage. In some organizations in Beijing, these expats—including people from Taiwan, Hong Kong, and Macau—add to the diversity of the workforce. These expats can usually speak Mandarin as well as another dialect of Chinese and a non-Chinese language such as English, but most do not speak Mandarin as a native dialect. They are not necessarily familiar with the communication style, business infrastructure, and culture found in Beijing.

Local employees expect these expats to have strong abilities in Mandarin, as well as a knowledge of Chinese culture and sensitivity to local conditions. In addition, local workers and non-Chinese expats often expect these expats of Chinese heritage to serve as "bridges" between operations outside of China and the local environment. Their ability to fulfill this "bridge role" depends on their sensitivity to local conditions in Beijing and their communication skills, among other factors.

While generally accepting of expats, one point of contention for local workers has to do with career development. Particularly in multinational corporations, local nationals often see their paths to professional advancement blocked by expats, whether foreign or of Chinese heritage. From their perspective, expats just seem to be replaced with more expats. Young local employees feel that they are stuck in jobs which offer no experience in managing others. It is important for managers and executives in foreign enterprises to understand and address these concerns.

Travel abroad is restricted, or at least very difficult to arrange, for many local employees in China. Expats whose presence is appreciated most by local people are those who effectively transfer knowledge and skills to local employees, and who act as liaisons and advocates for local people with the outside world.

There are many additional issues for expats working with local employees in Beijing. Differing communication styles can be an impediment to mutual understanding. Like so much else in Beijing, the business infrastructure is in a constant state of flux, requiring great flexibility from all concerned. Last but not least, there are many cultural differences among local workers and expats, which perhaps can be summed up using the Chinese expression *tong chuan yi meng* —"same bed, different dreams."

CONFIDENTIALITY AND PRIVACY

The issues of confidentiality and privacy are of great concern to many expats working in Beijing. Information that they assume is confidential and conversations that they believe are private tend to be discussed openly among local employees. There are several factors influencing these issues, some of which are cultural, some of which are influenced by economics, and others which are influenced by bureaucracy. It is wise for expats to be careful with information until they have learned some of the nuances of sharing it with others in Beijing.

In terms of culture, there is a tendency among Chinese people to share information with others on a nice-to-know basis, as well as to sort out matters of face and status and build or improve *guanxi*. Meetings are generally large gatherings so that everyone knows the gist of where business matters are headed. Salaries are discussed openly among Chinese people so that status is clear. A trade secret is leaked to an existing customer in order to curry favor, boost *guanxi* ties, and secure a large new sale. Conversely, people tend not to share negative information, as it can have an adverse impact on face, status, and *guanxi*.

In terms of economics, the strain on resources in China turns information into a type of currency, which is handled with great pragmatism. Valuable information is released in exchange for other valuable commodities, including intangible ones such as *guanxi* and face. Somewhat unique to China is the influence of bureaucracy, or more precisely the influence of government in business, which removes an element of individual control over business dealings. Feeling powerless in many situations, individuals regain a sense of control through their actions in acquiring and releasing information.

Communication styles can also influence the manner in which information is shared. With regard to written information, local people sometimes take their cue as to whether they should share it from the way the information is handled. For example, a fax received at the office is considered public information. It will probably be read several times before landing on the desk of the intended recipient. If it were confidential, would it have been sent to the company fax center? For this reason, most executives and managers have a private fax machine at home.

Similarly, they also take their cue from the manner in which information is shared orally. A Chinese manager might mention something loudly to a worker in order for others to "get the message" without having to inform them directly. Occasionally, a worker will be told that certain information is "confidential" precisely so that the worker will spread the news among others.

In essence, it is important for expats to know that the best way to keep written information private is to keep it on one's person at all times. The best way to share information confidentially is by discussing it with another person while walking down the street, surrounded by strangers. Until you learn the ropes, try to be cautious without being paranoid .

❀ ❀ ❀

Perhaps you can see why patience and stamina are the words heard most frequently to describe the characteristics required for outsiders to be successful working in Beijing. Despite the challenges, many find working in the city a satisfying and rewarding experience, as in many ways, doing business in the China market remains an exciting and open field.

Issues presented in this section comprise only a handful of the challenges experienced by outsiders who go to work in Beijing. There are plenty of good resources from which to learn more about these and other issues; a few sources are listed in the *Resource Guide*.

CULTURAL QUIZ

Here is a short quiz that will help you test your knowledge about the people and culture of Beijing. For each of these scenarios, there might be more than one appropriate response.

SITUATION ONE

You arrived in Beijing two days ago, and today is your first day of work. A colleague, a woman whom you met on a previous visit to the office, drops by your desk to talk. What should you do?

    A. Stand up to greet her and shake her hand. Remain standing as you talk.

    B. Do not shake her hand. Remain seated and ask her to sit down.

    C. Stand up to greet her and shake her hand. Ask her to sit down, and then offer to get her a cup of tea.

    D. Simply say *"Ni hao"* and go back to your work.

COMMENTS

It is customary among people in Beijing to stand and shake hands when they first meet, as well as after brief periods of separation. When colleagues visit your work area, you are considered a "host." A good host always stands to greet guests, invites them to sit down, and offers them a cup of tea. In this situation, gender and position in the hierarchy have little influence on behavior. (Your reaction to this situation will be different once you have settled into a daily routine. If you interact with this colleague regularly, standing for a handshake would not be necessary, but you should still ask her to sit down when she visits you at your desk. Offering a cup of tea is a nice gesture when you anticipate a prolonged conversation.)

SITUATION TWO

You wish to learn the proper way to pronounce the name of a Chinese person to whom you were introduced during a meeting, and wish to confirm which part of this person's name is the family name (surname). You ask a colleague for assistance, telling the colleague that the person's name was spelled "YAN ZHANG." Your colleague's answer to both of your questions is, "I don't know." What should you do now, and what is a likely explanation for your colleague's response?

- A. Show your colleague the person's business card so that your colleague can see the Chinese characters for the person's name. Otherwise, your colleague will not be able to help you.
- B. Ask someone else for assistance. Your colleague is obviously not very bright.
- C. The next time you see the person, ask again for pronunciation assistance and clarification. Chinese language is very difficult, even for native speakers.
- D. Double-check the spelling on the person's business card and try again. Perhaps you remembered the spelling incorrectly.

COMMENTS

When the sounds of Chinese words are spelled out in Roman letters, several problems arise. As there are many homonyms in Mandarin, it can be difficult to determine the corresponding Chinese characters. Also, although Chinese family names precede given names when written in characters, in romanized spelling people sometimes reverse the order of their names for the "benefit" of Westerners. Thus, it is not possible to determine which name is the family name simply from the sequence of the words. Whenever you need pronunciation assistance for Chinese names, it is best to show people the Chinese characters for those names.

SITUATION THREE

You are attending a formal banquet, and the person sitting next to you keeps putting food on your plate. The food is delicious, so you keep eating, but you are beginning to feel uncomfortable with this person's behavior. How should you react?

  A Tell this person that you are not an infant and that you can take care of yourself.
  B Accept the person's hospitality and say nothing.
  C Begin eating more slowly, leaving a bit of food on your plate at all times.
  D Start reciprocating by putting some food on that person's plate.

COMMENTS

A combination of three answers is actually the best reaction to this situation. Particularly at very formal banquets, members of the host party will try to be sure that you have food on your plate at all times. You should graciously accept the person's hospitality. Eat more slowly and leave some food on your plate. After the person serves you two or three times, you should reciprocate.

SITUATION FOUR

You are driving slowly along a small street in Beijing, looking for a building that you have not visited before. Suddenly you hear something scraping against the side of your car. Looking in the direction of the noise, you see a young man struggling with his bicycle. You stop the car and get out to investigate the situation and realize that he has put a half-meter-long scratch on your car. A few people from the neighborhood have started to gather around, and a couple of them begin talking with the bicyclist. Both he and the bicycle seem fine, and you notice that the bicyclist is laughing! How should you react?

- A. Show your anger to this guy by hollering. It's obvious that he is taking the situation, and the damage to your car, lightly.
- B. Realize that you were distracted and thus you might have played a role in the accident. Tell the young man that there is no problem, and leave.
- C. Leave quickly. Perhaps the crowd will turn against you because you are a foreigner.
- D. Call the traffic police immediately. Let them reprimand the young man appropriately.

COMMENTS

Laughter is sometimes a sign of nervousness or embarrassment. Be calm in this situation, especially because you could be at fault. The crowd will grow (out of curiosity) if you try to pursue the matter, so it is probably best to just get into your car and drive away if the bicyclist is not physically injured. Most Chinese people would not call the police for such a minor incident. Compensation for damages might be negotiated privately between you and the bicyclist if you speak Mandarin well and don't mind the crowds that this discussion will draw.

SITUATION FIVE

You have just returned home, and you notice that your young son has hives on his arm. Apparently, your *ayi* gave him some banana to eat. When you hired this *ayi*, you are certain that you told her not to feed your son any bananas, as he is mildly allergic. What should you do?

A Realize that your *ayi* is simply not very smart, and remind her not to give bananas to your son.

B Do not reprimand your *ayi*, as long as it seems that your son will recover from his hives.

C Fire the *ayi*. It is clear that she cannot follow simple instructions.

D Tell the *ayi* again not to feed bananas to your son, showing her the hives that he developed as a result of her actions.

COMMENTS

Although it is entirely possible that your *ayi* is not very smart, it is unlikely that this is the primary cause of her actions. It is more likely that your son was persistent about wanting some banana, and she thought that "just a little" couldn't hurt. Showing the *ayi* your son's hives will underline the seriousness of his condition. In any case, instructions to *ayis* should be reinforced regularly and frequently during their first few months of employment.

SITUATION SIX

You have just hailed a small taxi on the streets of Beijing, and you ask the driver to take you to the Friendship Store. He is looking at you with his eyebrows raised, and moves his shoulders upward seeming to signal that he needs more information. What should you do next?

A Give up on this driver and get another taxi.

B Show the driver the location of the Friendship Store you want to visit on a map.

C Report the driver's incompetence to the taxi company.
D Look in your pocket dictionary for the Chinese words for Friendship Store and try to pronounce them as best you can.

COMMENTS

With more than one Friendship Store in the city, it is important to point on a map to the one you want to visit. Although some smaller taxis are driven by newcomers who do not know the city well, even these drivers usually know where the Friendship Stores are located.

DO'S AND DON'TS APPENDIX

DO'S

Do have a basic knowledge of Beijing and its history to spice up conversations.

Do make an effort to learn and practice speaking Mandarin. You can improve only if you try.

Do be adventurous, exploring Beijing and its neighborhoods.

Do try Chinese foods that are new to you; even those that are exotic or unusual from your perspective.

Do remember the concept of "face." Learn how to give others face.

Do get used to the art of bargaining.

Do accept invitations to lunches and dinners from your Chinese hosts and be prepared to reciprocate.

Do prepare business cards in simplified Chinese characters and keep plenty of them with you at all times.

Do have tissues or toilet paper with you at all times.

Do maintain an open attitude and a sense of humor.

Do be reserved in your interactions with local people of the opposite gender.

Do be alert to physical hazards while walking on the streets of Beijing, as well as exercising caution when crossing them.

DON'TS

Don't make fun of or criticize Chinese people and their customs.

Don't isolate yourself from Chinese people by confining your life to the expatriate community.

Don't complain to local people about how "hard" your life is in Beijing.

Don't single out individuals for praise or blame.

Don't discuss politics or controversial topics.

Don't touch handrails or other places where Beijing's dust can gather. More importantly, don't touch your face until you have washed your hands!

Don't call Chinese people by their given names, unless and until you have been invited to do so.

Don't wear clothing that is overly garish or revealing.

Don't use your finger to point at anyone.

Don't blow your nose in the presence of people you know.

Don't drink tap water, eat uncooked vegetables, or take other unnecessary health risks.

Don't walk on the street while eating.

GLOSSARY

ROMANIZATION SYSTEMS

In the vocabulary lists that follow, we provide the *pinyin* romanized spellings with tone marks. For several years, *pinyin* has been the official system used in the PRC for transcribing the sounds of Mandarin using Roman letters. Many other systems of romanization are used around the world, including Yale (used primarily for Mandarin language teaching in the United States), and Wade-Giles (mostly used in Taiwan and for historical references).

TONES

In spoken Chinese, the meaning of a word changes when the speaker changes the tone in which the word is said. Please refer to the chapter on the *Chinese Language* for more information about the four tones used in Mandarin. Please note that wherever two syllables pronounced in the third tone occur in a row, such as in the name of the neighborhood, Wangfujing in speech, the tone of the first syllable is changed to a rising tone (second tone).

PRONUNCIATION GUIDE

Some sounds that occur in Mandarin have no equivalent in English. In combination with a **j**, **q**, or an **x**, or when written **ü**, the vowel **u** is pronounced as in the French word, tu. (For example, ju, qu, and xu.) The **h** sound in Mandarin is more raspy than in English and is more like the Spanish pronunciation of **j** in Jose. The pronunciation guide that follows gives approximations for the sounds of all other vowels and consonants, based on the pronunciation of standard (broadcast) American English. Review this guide carefully, as some syllables (such as *sheng*) might be pronounced quite differently from what you expect.

Vowels	Pronounce like:	Examples:
a	the **a** in father	*ma* (horse)
		mang (busy)
(except when following a **y**)		
a	the first **e** in ever	*yan* (salt)
(when following a **y**)		
ai	the **ai** in aisle	*ai* (love)
ao	the **ou** in outer	*hao* (good)
e	the **e** in oven	*he* (harmony)
(when it is the final sound in a syllable)		
e	the **u** in hung	*sheng* (life)
(when it is followed by an **r**, **ng**, or **n**)		
e	the **e** in yet	*ye* (leaf)
(when following a **y**)		
ei	the **ay** in day	*bei* (north)

i	the **ee** in seek	*ni* (you)
(when following a **b**, **d**, **j**, **l**, **m**, **n**, **p**, **q**, **t**, **x**, or **y**)		
i	**rr**	*shi* (ten)
(when following a **ch**, **r**, **sh**, or **zh**)		
i	the **e** in oven	*zi* (self)
(when following a **c**, **s**, or **z**)		
ia	the **ya** in yacht	*jia* (house)
		jiang (surname)
(when it is followed by **ng** or when it is the final sound in a syllable)		
ia	the **ye** in yet	*jian* (to build)
(when it is followed by an **n**)		
iao	the **yow** in yowl	*jiao* (to call)
ie	the **ye** in yet	*bie* (different)
io	the **you** in your	*xiong* (bear)
iu	the **you** in youth	*liu* (surname)
o	the **wa** in wart	*bo* (surname)
(when it is the final sound in a syllable)		
o	the **o** in open	*dong* (east)
(when it is followed by a consonant)		
ou	the **ow** in know	*kou* (mouth)
u	the **oo** in soon	*cu* (vinegar)
u	the **woo** in wood	*cun* (village)
(when it is followed by an **n**)		
ua	the **wa** in wander	*gua* (to hang)
(when following most consonants)		
ua	the **whe** in when	*yuan* (dollar)
(when following a **j**, **q**, **x**, or **y**)		
uai	why	*guai* (strange)
ue	yew-eh	*jue* (to decide)
ui	the **wei** in weigh	*gui* (expensive)
uo	the **wa** in water	*guo* (country)

Consonants	Pronounce like:	Examples:
c	the **ts** in cats	*cun* (inch)
ch	hard **ch**	*che* (vehicle)
	(using the back of the mouth)	
q	soft **ch**	*qing* (please)
	(using the front of the mouth)	
r	the **er** in ever	*ren* (person)
sh	hard **sh**	*ʃhao* (small quantity)
	(using the back of the mouth)	
x	**sy**, or soft **sh**	*xiao* (small size)
	(using the front of the mouth)	
z	the **ds** in bids	*zou* (to walk)
j	**j**	*jing* (capital)
	(using the front of the mouth)	
zh	**j**	*zhi* (to know)
	(using the back of the mouth)	

THE BASICS

English	Pinyin	Simplified Characters	Traditional Characters
Hello	nǐ hǎo ma?	你好吗	你好嗎
(less formal)	nǐ hǎo?	你好	你好
(most formal)	nín hǎo ma?	您好吗	您好嗎
Thank you	xìe xie	谢谢	謝謝
Where is the..	zài nǎr?	在哪儿	在哪兒
May I have ...please?	qǐng géi wǒ..	请给我	請給我
How much?	dūo shǎo qían?	多少钱	多少錢
(often pronounced by Beijingers as *∂uor qian*?)			
This one	zhè ge	这个	這個
(often pronounced *jei ge*)			

That one (often pronounced "nei ge")	nà ge	那个	那個
Goodbye	zài jìan	再见	再見
bathroom	xí shǒu jīan	洗手间	洗手間
man	nán	男	男
woman	nǔ	女	女

NUMBERS

English	Pinyin	Simplified Characters	Traditional Characters
zero	líng	零	零
one	yī	一	一
two	èr	二	二
two*	lǐang	两	兩
three	sān	三	三
four	sì	四	四
five	wǔ	五	五
six	lìu	六	六
seven	qī	七	七
eight	bā	八	八
nine	jǐu	九	九
ten	shí	十	十

* The alternate form for "two" (*liang*) is more frequently used than er. For example, to buy two apples, you would ask for *liang ge pingguo* instead of *er ge pingguo*. *Er* is mostly used when stating a series of digits such as a room number or telephone number.

A "NUMBER ONE" CHALLENGE

In most vocabulary lists, the standard translation for "one" is usually listed as *yi*. However, in standard Mandarin, a different term (*yao*) is used for "one" when stating a series of digits, such as when stating a room number or a telephone number. (This term is not used in all dialects of Chinese.) Its purpose is to avoid confusion with seven (*qi*), as *yi* rhymes with *qi*. Thus, if you want to tell a Chinese colleague that you are in room number 123, you should state the number as *yao er san* rather than *yi er san*.

one	yāo	幺	幺

PLACE NAMES AND TERMS — CHINA

English	Pinyin	Simplified Characters	Traditional Characters
province	shěng	省	省
Anhui	ān huī	安徽	安徽
Fujian	fú jìan	福建	福建
Gansu	gān sù	甘肃	甘肅
Guangdong	gǔang dōng	广东	廣東
Guizhou	gùi zhōu	贵州	貴州
Hainan	hǎi nán	海南	海南
Hebei	hé běi	河北	河北
Heilongjiang	hēi lóng jīang	黑龙江	黑龍江
Henan	hé nán	河南	河南
Hubei	hú běi	湖北	湖北
Hunan	hú nán	湖南	湖南
Jiangsu	jīang sū	江苏	江蘇
Jiangxi	jīang xī	江西	江西
Jilin	jí lín	吉林	吉林
Liaoning	líao níng	辽宁	遼寧

225

Qinghai	qīng hǎi	青海	青海
Shaanxi	shǎn xī	陕西	陝西
Shandong	shān dōng	山东	山東
Shanxi	shān xī	山西	山西
Sichuan	sì chūan	四川	四川
Taiwan	tái wān	台湾	臺灣
Yunnan	yún nán	云南	雲南
Zhejiang	zhè jīang	浙江	浙江
autonomous region	zì zhì qū	自治区	自治區
Guangxi	gǔang xī	广西	廣西
Inner Mongolia	nèi méng gǔ	内蒙古	內蒙古
Ningxia	níng xìa	宁夏	寧夏
Tibet	xī zàng	西藏	西藏
Xinjiang	xīn jīang	新疆	新疆
municipality	zì zhì shì	自治市	自治市
Beijing/ Peking	běi jīng	北京	北京
Chongqing	chóng qìng	重庆	重慶
Shanghai	shàng hái	上海	上海
Tianjin	tīan jīn	天津	天津
SAR*	tè bíe xíng zhèng qū	特别行政区	特別行政區
Hong Kong	xīang gǎng	香港	香港
Macau	aò mén	澳门	澳門

* Special Administrative Region

PLACE NAMES AND TERMS — BEIJING

English	Pinyin	Simplified Characters	Traditional Characters
Second Ring Road	èr húan lù	二环路	二環路
Third Ring Road	sān húan lù	三环路	三環路
gate	mén	门	們
outside	wài	外	外
inside	nèi	内	内
east	dōng	东	東
west	xī	西	西
north	běi	北	北
south	nán	南	南
Jianguo	jìan gúo	建国	建國
Chang An	cháng ān	长安	長安
avenue	dà jīe*	大街	大街

*Literally, *dajie* means "big street". Thus the term *jie* by itself means "street".

districts	qū	区	區
Changping	chāng píng	昌平	昌平
Chaoyang	cháo yáng	朝阳	朝陽
Chongwen	chóng wén	崇文	崇文
Daxing	dà xīng	大兴	大興
East City	dōng chéng	东城	東城
Fangshan	fáng shān	房山	房山
Fengtai	fēng tái	丰台	豐臺
Haidian	hǎi dìan	海淀	海澱
Mentougou	mén tóu gōu	门头沟	門頭溝

Shijingshan	shí jǐng shān	石景山	石景山
Shunyi	shùn yì	顺义	順義
Tongzhou	tōng zhōu	通州	通州
West City	xī chéng	西城	西城
Xuanwu	xūan wǔ	宣武	宣武
counties	xìan	县	縣
Huairou	húai róu	坏柔	懷柔
Miyun	mì yún	密云	密雲
Pinggu	píng gǔ	平谷	平谷
Yanqing	yán qìng	延庆	延慶

HISTORICAL NAMES AND PLACES

English	Pinyin	Simplified Characters	Traditional Characters
China	zhōng gúo	中国	中國
Zhoukoudian	zhōu kǒu dìan	周口店	周口店
Peking Man	běi jīng yúan rén	北京猿人	北京猿人
exhibition hall	zhǎn lán gǔan	展览馆	展覽館
Beiping	běi píng	北平	北平
Yanjing	yān jīng	燕京	燕京
Dadu	dà dū	大都	大都
Confucius Temple also known as	kǒng mìao	孔庙	孔廟
Capital Museum	shǒu dū bó wù gǔan	首都博物馆	首都博物館
"Forbidden City" also known as	gù gōng	故宫	故宫
Palace Museum	gù gōng bó wù gǔan	故宫博物馆	故宫博物館
Temple of Heaven	tīan tán gōng yúan	天坛公园	天壇公園

Great Wall	cháng chéng	长城	長城
Ming Tombs	shí sān líng	十三陵	十三陵
Jingshan Park	jǐng shān gōng yuán	景山公园	景山公園
Ancient Observatory	gǔ gūan xìang tái	古观象台	古觀象臺
Lama Temple	yōng hé gōng	雍和宫	雍和宮
Old Summer Palace	yúan míng yúan	圆明园	圓明園
Summer Palace	yí hé yúan	颐和园	頤和園

PHRASES

The following are the phrases mentioned in the chapter on the *Chinese Language*:

English	Pinyin	Simplified Characters	Traditional Characters
He has a book.	tā yǒu shū	他有书	他有書
I go.	wǒ qù	我去	我去
to want/will	yào	要	要
I want to/ will go	wǒ yào qù	我要去	我要去

NAMES AND TITLES

English	Pinyin	Simplified Characters	Traditional Characters
mister (Mr.)	xiān shēng	先生	先生
miss	xǐao jǐe	小姐	小姐
madame (Mme.)	nǚ shì	女士	女士
mistress (Mrs.)	tài tài	太太	太太
comrade	tóngzhì	同志	同志
master worker	shīfù	师傅	師傅

Some common Chinese family names (surnames) are:

Bo	bó	柏	柏
Chen	chén	陈	陳
Dai	dài	戴	戴
Fang	fáng	房	房
Guo	gūo	郭	郭
Han	hán	韩	韓
Jiang	jiāng	江	江
Kong	kǒng	孔	孔
Li	lǐ	李	李
Liu	líu	刘	劉
Ma	mǎ	马	馬
Mo	mò	莫	莫
Pan	pān	潘	潘
Sima	sī mā	司马	司馬
Song	sòng	宋	宋
Wang	wáng	王	王
Wu	wú	吴	吳
Xu	xú	徐	徐
Yang	yáng	杨	楊
Zhang	zhāng	张	張
Zhao	zhào	赵	趙

SUBWAY STOPS

There are no official translations for most of the names of Beijing subway stops. These names are colorful though, and a few hint at the past function of the old city gates. Some relatively literal translations of the subway stop names are offered below. (Names with asterisks (*) beside them are standard translations.)

English	Pinyin	Simplified Characters	Traditional Characters
Andingmen (Stability Gate)	ān dìng mén	安定门	安定門

Beijingzhan   běi jīng zhàn   北京站   北京站
(Beijing Station—the original Beijing railway station*)

Changchunjie   cháng chūn jīe   长椿街   長椿街
(Long Cedar Street)

Chaoyangmen   cháo yáng mén   朝阳门   朝陽門
(Facing Sunlight Gate)

Chegongzhuang   chē gōng zhūang 车公庄   車公莊
(Vehicles Public Manor)

Chongwenmen   chóng wén mén   崇文门   崇文門
(Lofty Culture Gate)

Dongdan   dōng dān   东单   東單
(East Unit)

Dongsishitiao   dōng sì shí tíao 东四十条 東四十條
(East Forty Strip)

Dongzhimen   dōng zhí mén   东直门   東直門
(East Straight Gate)

Gulou   gǔ lóu   鼓楼   鼓樓
(Drum Tower*)

Fuchengmen   fù chéng mén   阜成门   阜成門
(Abundant Success Gate)

Fuxingmen   fù xìng mén   复兴门   复興門
(Revival Gate)

Hepingmen   hé píng mén   和平门   和平門
(Harmony and Calm Gate or Peace Gate)

Jianguomen   jìan gúo mén   建国门   建國門
(Build Country Gate)

Jishuitan   jì shǔi tán   积水潭   積水潭
(Accumulated Water Pool)

Yonghegong   yōng hé gōng   雍和宫   雍和宫
(Lama Temple*)

Junshi   jūn shì
  Bowuguan   bó wù gǔan   军事博物馆 軍事博物官
(Military Museum*)

Muxidi (Wood Cassia Place)	mù xī dì	木樨地	木樨地
Nanlishi Lu (South Refined Scholar Road)	nán lǐ shì lù	南礼士路	南禮士路
Qianmen (Front Gate*)	qían mén	前门	前門
Tiananmen Dong (Heavenly Peace Gate East)	tīan ān mén dōng	天安门东	天安門東
Tiananmen Xi (Heavenly Peace Gate West)	tīan ān mén xī	天安门西	天安門西
Guo Mao (World Trade, i.e. China World Trade Center*)	gúo mào	国贸	國貿
Xidan (West Unit)	xī dān	西单	西單
Xizhimen (West Straight Gate)	xī zhí mén	西直门	西直門
Xuanwumen (Announce the Military Gate)	xūan wǔ mén	宣武门	宣武門
Yong An Li (Eternal Peace Neighborhood)	yǒng ān lǐ	永安里	永安里
Wangfujing (Prince's Mansion Well)	wáng fǔ jǐng	王府井	王府井

FOOD

English	Pinyin	Simplified Characters	Traditional Characters
beer	pí jǐu	啤酒	啤酒
coffee	kā fēi	咖啡	咖啡
tea	chá	茶	茶
cola	kě lè	可乐	可樂
meat	ròu	肉	肉
Peking Duck	běi jīng kǎo yā	北京烤鸭	北京烤鴨

rice (white; cooked)	mǐ fàn	米饭	米飯
tofu (bean curd)	dòu fǔ	豆腐	豆腐
vegetables	shū cài	蔬菜	蔬菜
water	shuǐ	水	水
Check, please.*	qǐng jíe zhàng	请结帐	請結帳

*Special note for people who speak Mandarin and are new to Beijing: Please do not ask for the *maidan*. Only outsiders do that!

SHOPPING

English	Pinyin	Simplified Characters	Traditional Characters
Wangfujing	wáng fǔ jǐng	王府井	王府井
Friendship Store	yǒu yì shāng dìan	友谊商店	友誼商店
"department selling small things"	xǐao mài bù	小卖部	小賣部
free market	zì yóu shì chǎng	自由市场	自由市場
Hua'an Meat Store (German butcher)	húa ān ròu dìan	华安肉店	華安肉店
Too expensive!	tài gùi	太贵	太貴

LEISURE

English	Pinyin	Simplified Characters	Traditional Characters
City Hotel	chéng shì bīn guǎn	城市宾馆	城市賓館

Confucius Temple also known as	kǒng mìao	孔庙	孔廟
Capital Museum	shǒu dū bó wù gǔan	首都博物馆	首都博物館
Imperial Academy	gǔo zǐ jìan	国子监	國子監
Jietai Temple	jìe tái sì	戒台寺	戒臺寺
Panjiayuan	pān jīa yúan	潘家园	潘家園
Temple of Earth	dì tán	地坛	地壇
Temple of Heaven	tīan tán	天坛	天壇
Temple of the Moon	yùe tán	月坛	月壇
Temple of the Sun	rì tán	日坛	日壇
Tanzhe Temple	tán zhè sì	潭柘寺	潭柘寺
Underground City	dì xìa chéng	地下城	地下城

MISCELLANEOUS

The following is an alphabetical list of other terms and phrases mentioned throughout this book:

English	Pinyin	Simplified Characters	Traditional Characters
acre (Chinese measure)	mǔ	亩	畝
banquet	yàn hùi	宴会	宴會
big nose	dà bí zi	大鼻子	大鼻子
center country speech	zhōng gúo hùa	中国话	中國話
center language	zhōng wén	中文	中文

Cheers! (literally, "dry glass")	gān bēi	干杯	乾杯
close enough	chà bù dūo	差不多	差不多
correct	dùi	对	對
country tongue	gúo yǔ	国语	國語
courtyard-style home	sì hé yùan	四合院	四合院
deep-breathing exercises	qì gōng	气功	氣功
foot (Chinese measure)	chǐ	尺	尺
foreigner	waì gúo rén	外国人	外國人
foreign guest	wài bīn	外宾	外賓
friend	péng yǒu	朋友	朋友
Han tongue	hàn yǔ	汉语	漢語
household helper	ā yí	阿姨	阿姨
inch (Chinese measure)	cùn	寸	寸
kilogram (one-half)	jīn	斤	斤
kilograms (50 kg)	dàn	担	擔
Mandarin (common speech)	pǔ tōng hùa	普通话	普通話
may I bother you	má fán nǐ	麻烦你	麻煩你
meters (3.3 m)	zhàng	丈	丈
money	qían	钱	錢
note (of currency)	yuán	元	元
officials' language	gūan hùa	官话	官話
old outsider	lǎo wài	老外	老外
one "cent"	fēn	分	分
outsider	wài dì rén	外地人	外地人
people's currency	rén mín bì	人民币	人民幣
piece (of money)	kuài	块	塊

please may I ask	qǐng wèn	请问	請問
relationship	gūan xi	关系	關係
residential lanes	hú tóng	胡同	胡同
rule of law	fǎ zhì	法治	法治
rule of person	rén zhì	人治	人治
shadow boxing	tài jí qúan	太极拳	太極拳
Silicon Valley (in China)	zhōng gūan cūn	中关村	中關村
spouse	ài rén	爱人	愛人
stick donuts (oily stick)	yóu tiáo	油条	油條
subway	dì tǐe	地铁	地鐵
tael (Chinese measure)	liǎng	两	兩
ten cents (written form)	jiǎo	角	角
ten cents (spoken form)	máo	毛	毛
thing	dōng xī	东西	東西
work unit	dān wèi	单位	單位

CALENDAR OF FESTIVALS AND HOLIDAYS

January 1	New Year's Day
January/February	Chinese New Year
March 8	International Women's Day
May 1	International Labor Day
October 1	National Day

In celebration of Chinese New Year (called "Spring Festival" in Chinese), most people travel to their hometowns to spend time with their families. Expats and Beijingers who have the option of avoiding travel during the week or so surrounding this holiday period generally do, as most modes of domestic transportation are booked solid. Some expats take the opportunity to travel

237

outside of China, but make reservations well in advance even for international trips. If you plan to stay in Beijing, you might want to visit one of the temples that holds celebrations—ask friends and colleagues for recommendations. Please note that many shops and stores are closed at this time.

As Chinese New Year is a lunar holiday, the date changes annually. For this holiday and for National Day, employees generally have three days off from work.

International Women's Day, March 8, is not celebrated with as much fanfare as in some other countries; nevertheless, women are given the afternoon off.

Many foreign companies also give their employees time off for holidays celebrated in the company home office. For example, an Italian company might give workers the day off on December 25 for Christmas, even though it is not celebrated in China.

It is important to note that, around the time of certain holidays and special events, the movement of people and vehicles are often restricted within the city limits of Beijing. If you are making holiday plans that might be affected by such restrictions, be sure to check with local friends and colleagues for details a few days in advance.

RESOURCE GUIDE

CHINESE LANGUAGE RESOURCES

For people who wish to begin learning Mandarin before leaving for China, there is an abundance of resources at their disposal. One of the most comprehensive selections in English is available from China Books & Periodicals in San Francisco, USA. Contact them at tel: 1-415-282-2994, fax: 1-415-282-0994, or by email at info@chinabooks.com.

For those who prefer to use their computer to learn Mandarin, we recommend the Rosetta Stone CD-Rom program produced by Fairfield Language Technologies. This program is also available in other languages, and can be purchased at large computer stores in some countries or through their website at http://www.rosettestone.com. If either your time or your budget is limited, or if you would like to see if your learning style is compatible with the methodology, try the "Chinese (Mandarin) Explorer" available from sources such as Amazon.com. This abbreviated version offers the first 22 (out of 210) lessons of the full Rosetta Stone course.

Phrase Books

Scott D. Seligman and I-Chuan Chen. (2001). *Barron's Chinese at a Glance.* Happauge, NY/USA: Barron's Educational Series. Useful features of this book include a short description of some aspects of Chinese culture and brief guidelines on getting around the country, as well as a mini-dictionary. Some phrases offered in this book, however, are a bit stilted and wordy. When purchased in the United States, the book usually comes with a cassette tape for pronunciation practice. Too tall and heavy to actually carry in a pocket, the book is still small enough to carry in a purse or backpack.

Dr. Cheng Ma et al. (1998). *Berlitz Mandarin Chinese Phrasebook and Dictionary.* Princeton, NJ/USA: Berlitz Publishing Company, Inc. This phrasebook is compact and conveniently laid out, but the pronunciations of Chinese characters are presented in a unique style of romanization that might not be helpful for all readers. People planning long-term residency in Beijing might find the itemized lists of vocabulary for bicycle and car parts useful.

Dr. Nancy Duke Láy. (1980). *Say It in Chinese (Mandarin).* New York, NY/USA: Dover Publications. Smaller than some other "pocket" guides, it is possible to carry this one with you as you roam Beijing. However, there are a few drawbacks. As this guide uses Yale romanization only, it is really most helpful for native speakers of American English. While the book contains Chinese characters that you could point to in order to show someone what you are trying to say, the characters are traditional ones that many younger people in China have difficulty reading.

PREDEPARTURE CROSS-CULTURAL TRAINING

If you are moving to Beijing for a large company or organization, ask your employer to provide a few days of cross-cultural training before you depart. It will add much to the knowledge you have gained by reading this book. Cross-cultural training firms usually provide background on China and Chinese culture, an introduction to the Chinese (Mandarin) language, and other guidance according to your function. Most can even provide an introduction for children over the age of eight or so. Here is a list of some organizations in the United States that provide this type of training:

The Brannen Group
1240 Sixth Street, Suite C, Berkeley, CA 94710;
tel: 510-225-0093; http://www.brannengroup.com;
email: brannengrp@aol.com; fax: 510-225-0096

Cendant Intercultural, The Bennett Group
Civic Opera Building, 20 North Wacker Drive, Suite 1600,
Chicago, Illinois 60606; tel: 312-251-9000;
http://www.cendantintercultural.com;
email: consult@cendantintercultural.com; fax: 312-251-9015

Cornelius Grove & Associates, LLC
442 Forty-Seventh Street, Brooklyn, New York 11220-1216;
tel: 718-492-1896; http://www.grovewell.com;
email: info@grovewell.com; fax: 718-492-4005

Global Dynamics Inc.
19 Wilkinson Road, Randolph, New Jersey 07869;
tel: 973-927-9135; http://www.global-dynamics.com;
email: info@global-dynamics.com; fax: 973-927-6936

IOR (International Orientation Resources) Global Services
500 Skokie Boulevard, Suite 600, Northbrook, Illinois 60062;
tel: 847-205-0066; http://www.iorworld.com;
email: info@iorworld.com; fax: 847-205-0085

Meridian Resources Associates
1741 Buchanan Street, San Francisco, California 94115;
tel: 415-749-2920; http://www.meridianglobal.com;
email: info@meridianglobal.com; fax: 415-749-0124

Prudential Relocation International
2555 55th Street, Boulder, Colorado 80301; tel: 303-430-1076;
http://www.prudential.com/prm/products/rmpzz1004.html

Training Management Corporation
600 Alexander Road, Princeton, New Jersey 08540;
tel: 609-951-0525; http://www.tmcorp.com;
email: info@tmcorp.com; fax: 609-951-0395

Witham & Associates
677 Bounty Drive, Suite 204, Foster City, California 94404;
tel: 650-349-5920; email: withamassociates@aol.com

EXECUTIVE COACHING

Some of the firms that provide cross-cultural training, such as
Cornelius Grove & Associates, Meridian Resources, and Witham
& Associates, also provide one-on-one executive coaching. Such
services are also provided by:

CSC Consulting Limited
G.P.O. Box 712, Hong Kong
tel: 852-2522-6071; email: maurafallon@cscconsulting.com.hk;
fax: 852-2522-8967

George Renwick
P.O. Box 5007, Trade Center, Carefree, Arizona 85377 USA;
tel: 480-488-9566

RESOURCES IN BEIJING

There are so many resources for expats living in Beijing that it would be impossible to list them all. Check at some of the restaurants, hotels, and office buildings that cater to foreigners to find English-language magazines that list telephone numbers, meeting times, meeting locations, and other details.

- The International Network of Newcomers meets monthly. Look for announcements of their meetings in embassy newsletters and grocery stores catering to foreigners.
- All foreigners in Beijing should maintain contact with their embassies. The embassies of different countries sometimes sponsor events that are open to all expats. Check for listings and contact the embassies with any questions.
- There are several foreign chambers of commerce in Beijing that host regular meetings. These meetings can provide newly arrived businesspeople the contacts they need to get off to a good start. Ask representatives in the commercial section of your country's embassy if there is a chamber of commerce supporting companies from your home country.
- Rotarians meet once a month in Beijing. Get the meeting times and dates from the online newsletter *Xianzai Beijing* or from one of the English-language publications distributed around the city.

EMERGENCIES

Emergency numbers can be accessed from any telephone, including mobile telephones, toll free. In Beijing, the emergency numbers to call are:

Police	110	Call for most types of emergencies even when you are simply lost.
Fire	119	
Traffic Police	122	

243

WEBSITES ON BEIJING

GENERAL
About China
http://www.gochina.about.com
The main website contains sections on several countries in.
Information available in the "China" section ranges from business
directories to geography.

Beijing Municipal Government
http://www.beijing.gov.cn/english
Visit this website for official news from China's capital city. You
can also find links to other government organizations as well as to
official publications.

Beijing Page
http://www.beijingpage.com
Information on Beijing's tourism, industry, and entertainment are
covered on this comprehensive website. Under "Beyond Beijing"
is a list of websites of particular interest to expats.

China Today
http://www.chinatoday.com
Exploring this extensive website could take hours. Visitors can
select from a wide range of topics, including a few not generally
found elsewhere (such as "social science").

Greatest Cities (Beijing)
http://www.greatestcities.com
Selecting Asia, then China and finally Hebei Province leads visitors
to a concise overview of Beijing. Presented as items in an
encyclopedia, the essays are self-contained and do not provide
links to other websites.

BUSINESS SERVICES

Beijing E-C Translation Ltd.
http://www.e-cchina.com
Beijing E-C Translation Ltd. is a translation and localization service provider. Offerings include software and website localization and testing, as well as technical, marketing, and multimedia document translation in English, Japanese, German, French, and Chinese (simplified and traditional).

Beijing Translation Network
http://www.transnetwork.com.cn/english
This organization offers translation and interpreting services for a wide range of languages, such as English, French, German, Italian, Spanish, Romanian, Russian, Japanese, Korean, Thai, Polish, Dutch, Arabic, Vietnamese, and Mongolian. The Beijing office is open 24 hours a day, seven days a week.

China Business World
http://www.cbw.com
Covering multiple business categories from retail to media to employment, this website is one-stop shopping for business visitors to China. The latest edition of *Business Beijing* can be accessed from the "Business" section. Information on travel and shopping is available as well.

China Council for the Promotion of International Trade (CCPIT)
www.ccpit.org
Hosted in combination with the China Chamber of International Commerce, statistics, details of exhibitions, and other information can be found on this official website.

China Exporter

http://www.chinaexporter.net

Click on "Beijing" for lists of companies, government agencies, hotels, and universities located in the capital. The languages of the linked websites vary: some are in English, some in Chinese, and others are bilingual.

EDUCATION
Beijing BISS International School

http://www.biss.com.cn

Serving over 300 students from 40 different countries, this school consists of a Lower School (kindergarten to Grade 5) and Upper School (Grades 6–12). The website provides information about the curriculum, faculty, and history of the school,

The Beijing Center

http://www.thebeijingcenter.org

Formed by a consortium of Jesuit universities and colleges, this undergraduate institution offers courses in Chinese language, culture, and business. The center also conducts field trips to various areas of special interest in China, such as the Silk Road.

Columbia University Summer Sessions

http://www.columbia.edu

From this website, look for information on summer programs overseas to learn details about Columbia's Chinese language program. Delivered on the campus of Qinghua (Tsinghua) University, the summer sessions are supplemented by activities such as group excursions in and around Beijing.

Peking University

http://www.pku.edu.cn/eindex

Practical information concerning the campus and courses available to students can be found on this website of one of Beijing's foremost institutes of higher learning.

Western Academy of Beijing
http://www.wab.edu
Founded in 1994, this was the second international school to be located in Beijing. The Western Academy's academic program runs from nursery school through Grade 8.

EMBASSIES
British Embassy in Beijing
http://www.britishembassy.org.cn

Canadian Embassy
http://www.canada.org.cn

Foreign Embassies in Beijing
http://www.embassyworld.com
This website provides addresses and contact information for the embassies of many countries located in cities around the world, including Beijing.

Indian Embassy in Beijing
http://www.chinaembassy-india.org

U.S. Embassy in Beijing
http://www.usembassy-china.org.cn

LIFESTYLE
Baguazhang (A Chinese Martial Art)
http://www.beijingbagua.com
One particular style of Chinese martial art is introduced here – Beijing Baguazhang (Eight Trigrams Palm). The website explains

this type of martial art and provides a history of martial arts and links to related events and articles.

Beijing American Club
http://www.amerclubil.com
Select "Beijing" to learn more about the Beijing American Club, designed to satisfy the commercial, social, and recreational needs of business executives and their families.

Beijing Guide
http://www.beijingguide.com
A distinctive feature of this website is a message forum where expats can seek and exchange information and advice on life in China. Additional features include photographs of Beijing and useful telephone numbers.

Beijing Restaurants
http://www.travel.com.hk
A Beijing restaurant guide can be found under "Beijing" within this website. It offers an extensive list of restaurants specializing in various cuisines (even relatively rare ones, such as Muslim, Mongolian, Dai, and vegetarian), as well as restaurants serving foreign food. Although names of restaurants are provided, unfortunately addresses and telephone numbers are not.

Beijing Tai-Chi & Kung Fu Academy
http://www.beijingkungfu.com
An introduction to the Beijing Tai Chi and Kung Fu Academy is provided on this website. It includes descriptions of various courses in Tai Chi Chuan *(taijiquan)* and Kung Fu *(gongfu)*, as well as fees and schedules.

Beijing This Month Online
http://cbw.com/btm
This monthly publication gives expats and visitors access to what is going on in Beijing. Topics covered include fashion, travel, dining, and expat life.

Canadians in China
http://www.canadiansinchina.com
Canadians residing in China can use this website as a resource for information about community events and activities.

The Capital Club
http://www.thecapitalclub.com
The Capital Club was designed as a private club offering business, athletic, and social activities for executives. The website provides an introduction to the club facilities and a calendar of events.

Expats in China
http://www.expatsinchina.com
Much useful and interesting information to enrich the lives of expats living in China is available on this website. Topics covered include health care, housing, sports, and transportation.

Kehillat Beijing
http://www.sinogogue.org
Social and religious activities for the Jewish community in Beijing are listed here. It includes special events and holidays, as well as information about the community softball team called Pinyin Minyan.

Sports Beijing
http://www.sportsbeijing.com
Sports Beijing provides athletic programs for the youth of Beijing.

Its members include over 600 children from ages three to 18, representing 42 nationalities from schools all over Beijing. Activities include soccer, rugby, tennis, gymnastics, ice-hockey, horseback-riding, baseball, and roller-hockey.

Xianzai Beijing
http://www.xianzai.com
Xianzai means "Now" in Mandarin, so this website is a good source of up-to-date information on happenings in Beijing. Visit it to subscribe to free newsletters and get details on a wide range of topics, such as cultural events, health and fitness, and restaurants.

NEWS
Beijing Globe
http://www.beijingglobe.com
This site covers world news and current events with an emphasis on China and Asia, including special sections on Asia News and Asia Business.

Beijing News.Net
http://thebeijingnews.net
Business and financial news are covered on this website, including reports from China and other parts of Asia. It also provides links to additional Chinese news sources such as Beijing Globe and the People's Daily.

Beijing Review
http://www.bjreview.com.cn
This online edition of the English-language magazine *Beijing Review* offers local, domestic, and international news highlights.

China.org.cn
http://www.china.org.cn/english

Billed as "China's Official Gateway to News," visitors can select from a variety of categories for news and information. Some of the topics covered range from cooking to press conferences.

People's Daily
http://english.peopledaily.com.cn
A full array of news coverage from the China perspective is provided by this English-language version of the *People's Daily*. Useful links offer access to the websites of Chinese organizations and translations of official documents.

Zhaodaola (Found It!)
http://english.zhaodaola.com
Zhaodaola offers much in the way of news and information about China. There are several interesting categories to choose from, such as careers, education, the environment, health, living in China, real estate, statistics, and travel.

TRAVEL
China International Travel Service
http://www.cits.net
From this website, China's premier travel provider offers a comprehensive array of information and services for destinations all over China, including Beijing.

China Travel Guide
http://www.travelchinaguide.com
This Chinese website provides information about Beijing and other cities around the country from a variety of angles. Maps, lists of restaurants, and useful numbers for emergencies are found here.

China Travel System
http://www.chinats.com

General travel information for most areas of China is available from this main website. Under "Destination Guide," specific locations such as Beijing are covered in detail.

CNN City Profile Beijing
http://www.cnn.com
Information on Beijing can be found in the travel section of CNN's main website. It covers the usual topics, including places to visit, dine, and shop, and includes access to a handy currency converter.

Lonely Planet (Beijng)
http://www.lonelyplanet.com/destinations
Choosing Beijing as your destination will give you access to basic travel information about the city. One interesting feature is "Off the Beaten Track," which mentions sites most tourists never visit such as the Underground City and the Simatai section of the Great Wall of China.

FURTHER READING

A good source of written information about other cultures is the Intercultural Press in Yarmouth, Maine, U.S. Here you can find books on Chinese culture, as well as on more general subjects such as moving and adjusting to a new culture. Contact them at tel: 1-207-846-5168, fax: 1-207-846-5181, or visit their website at http://www.interculturalpress.com.

If you cannot find titles listed in this section at your favorite local bookstore, you will probably be able to order them from an online supplier such as Amazon.com.

BEIJING GUIDEBOOKS

M.Q. (1997). *Beijing*. Beijing: Foreign Languages Press. Available at most bookstores and gift shops, this book offers information about Beijing from the perspective of an outsider—the author is originally from Suzhou (a city near Shanghai). Certain information is included in this book that one cannot find in most other writings on Beijing: listings of obscure temples; details for getting around on the bus system; and a star rating system that highlights the best sites. Some parts of this book, though, do not take into account the special needs of foreigners—for example, *pinyin* Romanizations are not offered for all place names and addresses, and tones are included only in the vocabulary list at the back of the book.

Brian McClain (Editor). (1998). *The Beijing Guidebook*. Beijing: Middle-Kingdom Press. For three years, expat guides were published by different groups in Beijing. This was the third one to be published, and it is a shame that no updates have been produced. Covering topics that other books don't, such as housing, technology, and night life, this guide is quite handy to have around although some details are outdated. It can be hard to find—look in hotel gift shops in Beijing to see if you can spot a copy, or contact China Books & Periodicals (email: info@chinabooks.com) to see if they still have any copies left in stock.

Tom Le Bas (Editor). (2000). *Insight Guide: Beijing*. Singapore: APA Publications GmbH & Co. Reading this book is a great way for English speakers to get a feel of the city. The layout of the book presents aspects of culture and different areas of the city in a well-organized fashion, and the photographs of people and places are beautiful. A huge drawback for Chinese speakers, though, is that the book does not offer Chinese characters for any of the place names mentioned in the text, nor does it offer the tones for *pinyin* Romanizations. Some useful vocabulary is included in the back covering the basics such as greetings and food.

Caroline Liou and Robert Storey. (2001). *Lonely Planet Beijing*. Victoria, Australia: Lonely Planet Publications Pty Ltd. It is amazing how much information is packed into this relatively small guide to such a big city. Most listings are accompanied by the site names in both Chinese characters and *pinyin* with tones. The book includes cultural explanations, fairly useful maps, and snapshots that add flavor to the written descriptions. True to form, lots of tips are offered for budget-conscious travelers. If you want just one guide to use, this should probably be it.

CHINESE CULTURE

Hu Wenzhong and Cornelius Grove. (1999). *Encountering the Chinese: A Guide for Americans*. Yarmouth, ME/USA: Intercultural Press, Inc. This book is an excellent introduction to Chinese culture. Although intended primarily for Americans, it can also be useful to Westerners from other countries. Matters of etiquette and protocol are covered, but these writers are at their best when presenting deeper cultural issues such as "face" and modesty. The second part of the book is devoted to general issues encountered while living and working in China.

Scott Seligman. (1999). *Chinese Business Etiquette: A Guide to Protocol, Manners, and Culture in the People's Republic of China*. New York, NY/USA: Warner Books, Inc. The intricacies of forming and maintaining relationships with people in China can be complex, but this book is an excellent primer for the business setting. Greetings, meetings, and banquets are all covered in a fair amount of detail. Also included in this book are revealing anecdotes to illustrate cultural points.

Mayfair Mei-hui Yang. (1994). *Gifts, Favors, and Banquets: The Art of Social Relationships in China*. Ithaca, NY/USA: Cornell University Press. Meant to be a scholarly work, this book is an essential read for those who must know the finest points about building relationships with Chinese people. In fact, the Chinese

255

title of the book includes the term *guanxi* (*guanxi xue*, meaning the "study of guanxi"). It could also be of particular interest to students of Chinese culture who would like to know how traditional notions of *guanxi* operate in China today.

LIVING IN CHINA

Bill Holm. (1990). *Coming Home Crazy.* Minneapolis, MN/USA: Milkweed Editions. Holm organized this book as an "Alphabet of China Essays." Although Holm spent his time in Xi'an rather than Beijing—Xi'an being a smaller but no less noble city—it is still a good idea to read this book before moving to China. The essays recount his personal experiences in putting American and Chinese culture in perspective. His various tales of getting to know Chinese people and their culture are often poignant and sometimes hilarious.

Christine Hall. (1996). *Living & Working in China: How To Obtain Entry and Plan a Successful Stay.* Plymouth/UK: How To Books Ltd. Written by a teacher who was posted to a remote town in northeastern China, this is a very general guide to living in China. In particular, people who will be teaching in Beijing might find certain portions of this book worthwhile. A rather nice feature is the inclusion of real-life vignettes and personal accounts. Although some of the information applies more to life in the hinterlands than to life in Beijing, it could be very useful to expats who plan to travel to less developed areas of China during the course of their stay.

Rebecca Weiner, Margaret Murphy, and Albert Li. (1997). *Living in China: A Guide to Teaching & Studying in China, including Taiwan and Hong Kong.* San Francisco: China Books & Periodicals, Inc. First published in 1991, this book is useful for anyone who is interested in learning more about the educational system in China. General recommendations concerning adjustment and working within Chinese institutions of learning are covered, but perhaps the most helpful section for teachers and students is the directory of schools and other resources in the back of the book.

CHINA BUSINESS

Jim Mann. (1997). *Beijing Jeep: A Case Study of Western Business in China*. Boulder, CO/USA: Westview Press. Originally published in 1989, this book is highly readable and a great introduction to the history of one American company's operations in China. Although many details are outdated, it is amazing just how much of what American Motors experienced still holds true for foreign companies today. In particular, the story highlights the pitfalls of typical American style, senior-level executive thinking about the China market. Some issues presented, such as the handling of media and public relations, are not dealt with in most other books about doing business in China.

Huang Quanyu, Ph.D., Joseph Leonard, Ph.D., and Chen Tong. (1997). *Business Decision Making in China*. Binghamton, NY/ USA: The Haworth Press, Inc. Although certain parts of this book are already outdated, it provides a glimpse at the multiple facets of individual and institutional decision-making in Chinese enterprises. Cultural factors as well as the impact of bureaucracies and government structure on commercial enterprises are addressed. Some of the information included here can be obtained from other sources, but this is one of the only published works that pulls everything together in a coherent way. Explanations can be complex and confusing in places, but then, so can Chinese decision-making practices.

Conghua Li. (1998). *China: The Consumer Revolution*. Singapore: John Wiley & Sons (Asia) Pte Ltd. Those who would like to know more about consumer habits and spending patterns in China will find this book insightful. Figures in several statistical tables end with 1994 or 1995, and only projected figures for 2000 are provided, but this shortcoming is balanced by the author's obvious familiarity with the Chinese system and the consumers of modern China.

HISTORY

Chinese text by Weng Li, English translation by Mai Yangzeng. (1994). *Hutongs of Beijing*. Beijing: Beijing Arts and Photography Publishing House. Beautifully illustrated with black and white photographs, this book describes the history of Beijing's *hutongs*. The *hutong* (along with the *siheyuan*) were part of the grand design of the city that originated in the Yuan and Ming dynasties. The book describes how political changes in the country and the city were reflected in the *hutong*, including their size and distribution. Origins of some of the names of the *hutong* are also introduced.

Chinese text by Ma Bingjian, English translation by Mai Yangzeng. (1994). *Quadrangles of Beijing*. Beijing: Beijing Arts and Photography Publishing House. Color photographs illustrate this history of "quadrangles" or courtyard homes (*siheyuan*) showing how, from inception to the Yuan dynasty, they were part of the grand design of the city, along with the *hutong*. The book describes how certain architectural and decorative features reflect cultural traditions and provide an indication of the social status of the occupants. As in *Hutongs of Beijing*, the photographs constitute the main feature of the book, illustrating the distinctive features of the *siheyuan*.

Susan Naquin. (2000) *Peking: Temples and City Life, 1400–1900*. Berkeley: University of California Press. In this book, the author captures the feeling of life in Beijing during the Ming and Qing dynasties by studying the temples of Beijing. Temples served as centers of various community activities, such as fairs and markets. The formation of the capital in the Ming dynasty is described, as well as the transformation of the city with the Manchu conquest and the establishment of the Qing dynasty, a traumatic experience for Chinese residents.

Joanna Waley-Cohen. (1999). *The Sextants Of Beijing: Global Currents in Chinese History*. New York: W.W. Norton Paperback. Dispelling the myth of an isolationist, monolithic China impervious to foreign influences, Joanna Waley-Cohen traces China's history of foreign relations from the Han Dynasty to the present. Her writings describe China's continuous contact with foreign countries and peoples, and demonstrate China's pragmatic and open attitude in borrowing and using foreign ideas. It also shows that China has been continuously reshaped and changed through such contacts. The word "sextants" in the title refers to the astronomical instruments built by the Jesuits for the Qing court. These instruments can be found atop the Ancient Observatory in Beijing, serving as a symbol of China's interest in Western cultures.

ABOUT THE AUTHORS

Kay Jones holds a degree in Chinese studies and French language from the State University of New York at Albany. Originally from the U.S., she lived in Beijing for three years and continues to travel there frequently. She has also lived in France, England, and Japan. Her professional background includes work in the fields of international trade, not-for-profit, and retail, with over a dozen years spent consulting on global business practices and intercultural issues. She has traveled around China as well as to Singapore, Canada, Italy, and Germany, and speaks Mandarin, French, and some Japanese in addition to her native English. Although she has written several articles on foreign businesses operating in China, this is her first book.

Anthony Pan was born in China and educated in Hong Kong and the U.S. He completed graduate studies in sociology and East Asian studies at Princeton University and in Chinese history at the University of California at Berkeley, going on to teach East Asian sociology and history at Sophia University in Tokyo. Later, he conducted research in Chinese history as a Fulbright Fellow at Tokyo University. He holds a law degree from Columbia University, and is a member of the New York Bar. For several years he has worked as a consultant, traveling frequently to Beijing and other Chinese cities to advise on international business and cultural issues. He speaks Cantonese, Mandarin, English, and Japanese.

INDEX